THE BOLD NEW NORMAL

Creating the Africa where everyone prospers

Lucy Quist

The Bold New Normal

Creating the Africa where everyone prospers

Dakpabli & Associates
Accra

THE BOLD NEW NORMAL –
CREATING THE AFRICA WHERE EVERYONE PROSPERS

ISBN: 978-9988-2-9449-6

Editorial Team
Nana Awere Damoah
Kofi Akpabli
Amma Ampong Agyeman-Prempeh

Cover design by Nana Abban, Invictüs

Book Layout by multiPIXEL Limited
P O Box DC 1965, Dansoman, Accra, Ghana
Tel: +233 302 333 502 | +233 246 725 060 | +233 246 210 862

Published by
DAkpabli & Associates
P O Box 7465, Accra North, Accra, Ghana
Tel: +233 264 339 066 | +233 244 704 250 | +233 247 896 375
Email: info@dakpabli.com

ABOUT THE AUTHOR

Lucy Quist is an international business leader, author and distinguished global speaker on leadership, business and technology who believes that it is possible to deliberately create prosperous futures for marginalised societies around the world.

She particularly believes that in this time, Africa has the chance to raise a generation of young people who will create a new continent built on bold visions.

She is the first Ghanaian woman to head a multinational telecommunications company as the former CEO of Airtel Ghana. She is a co-founder of the Executive Women Network in Ghana.

Lucy is a chartered electrical and electronic engineer with an MBA from INSEAD and a First Class Honours degree from the University of East London. She is a member of the Institute of Engineering and Technology (UK).

She is a passionate advocate who believes in harnessing Science, Technology, Engineering and Mathematics (STEM) to advance development in Africa. She also advocates for greater participation in STEM especially for young people across the continent.

Lucy is committed to empowering young people across the African continent to fully realise their potential. In response to young people, she started writing in 2014 to engage, inspire and empower the next generation of African leaders.

Please visit www.lucyquist.com to learn more about Lucy's work.

DEDICATION

This book is dedicated to the people who set me on this path and have sustained me.

To my father, the intellectual who taught me to be bold and own my voice!

To my mother, the dreamer who taught me to dream beyond what I can see!

To my husband, the visionary who sees purpose long before anyone else does!

To my children, the generation that inspires me to bequeath a better world!

The right people have always been there…

ACKNOWLEDGEMENTS

Thank you to the many young people who approached me and asked me to mentor them. They challenged me to think of ways to reach many more people despite obvious limitations of time and location. Sitting round a table with a team of trusted people, we agreed there was only one way forward – connect with young people through media that they use.

That is how my Facebook page, Lucy Quist, was born in December 2014. My writing is a response to the need to connect, share lessons and sustain the belief that future generations will find hope to inspire them to their own greatness.

We have walked this journey together as they have read and provided feedback that I have diligently read and learnt from to enrich my thinking. Their push, gently and gradually, turned me into a writer. We have made progress together.

This book is the product of that gradual process. A process of consistency and continuous refinement!

We made it!

I was overjoyed when Patrick agreed to write the foreword. His work epitomises what is possible - a great vision being executed for a prosperous new Africa! Medaase.

I have learnt that writing a book is about more than great ideas and good diction. There is a painstaking process behind getting it right. Team DAkpabli made that process possible and I am proud that I could work with a professional publishing house right here in Ghana!

Thank you all. My teams complete me!

Most importantly, thank you heavenly Father for inspiration, ordered steps and grace.

CONTENTS

FOREWORD

I believe in the notion of a Bold New Normal for Africa. With population growth that eclipses other regions of the world, and that promises to double Africa's population within a generation, nothing short of a Bold New Normal is required for the future prosperity and wellbeing of Africans.

The coming demographic shift will stress all systems on the continent: health care, agriculture, education, infrastructure, law and order, and the availability of jobs. It will also present a tremendous opportunity for the provision of goods and services for this growing market.

Our vision at Ashesi University, in Ghana, is to educate the young leaders of this continent to be agents of the transformation that Africa needs – to be agents of a bold, new, positive normal. Our approach involves shaping the mindset, skillset and character of our students. And our experience shows that the bold new normal that Lucy talks about is feasible, especially with a younger generation that is open to exploring the possibilities before us.

However, it can be easy to miss the woods for the trees; and with the immediate challenges around us, it can sometimes seem as if our actions cannot have a big enough impact. It is important that we keep reminding ourselves and this generation not to accept this status quo or settle into the idea that a renewed Africa is not within reach. It is. And I hope that everyone who reads this book is inspired to keep pressing on, especially the young leaders around the continent who we now look to safeguard our future.

Patrick G. Awuah, Jr, Founder and President of Ashesi University, Ghana

THE EVOLUTION OF THE BOLD NEW NORMAL – A RINGSIDE VIEW

It felt like any other late Monday afternoon, except that, for some reason, it was unusually warm; and traffic was building up rather early. I was standing by the window in my office on the fourth floor of the GNAT Heights building overlooking the Independence Avenue. I had taken a break, something I do often when I crave some inspiration after hours at my desk drafting a communication strategy, reviewing a presentation or a media release. On this particular occasion, I was finalising the communication strategy for the business ahead of the 2017 financial year. As Head of Corporate Communications for Airtel Ghana at the time, I worked very closely with Lucy. My office separated from hers only by a meeting room to the right. I was a little over a year in my role whilst Lucy was barely three years in her position as chief steward of the fastest growing telecommunications business in Ghana.

Very early on when I joined the company, Lucy and I struck a great working relationship. She inspired me with her bold, almost idealistic vision – not only for the company but for a prosperous African continent anchored on unlocking the potential of young people. As a young person, I was sold on her ideas and would eventually become her de-facto sounding board and her brand and communication advisor.

"Richard! Richard!"

I turned from the scene of construction workers putting finishing touches to a couple of high-rise structures across the street opposite our office and the unfolding vehicular traffic just as Lucy walked into my office, more excited than when I had seen her a couple of hours earlier.

"I just figured the perfect title for the TedxEuston Talk. I think I will call it the **New Normal,"** she said, more out of conviction than a suggestion. We had been discussing and prepping towards her second Tedx talk, already on the fifth draft of her presentation; clear on the message but not yet on a title.

"That sounds great Lucy!" I responded. Not sure at the time where the inspiration for the title came from but well accustomed to the way Lucy's mind works on such matters, I was certain she had thought deeply about this or was being inspired by some external stimuli.

We spent the next forty-five minutes rethinking the purpose of the talk and the outcome we sought. By the time we were done, it was clear to both of us that there was a call to ***boldness*** in this ***New Normal***. The talk was going to be a charge! A call to action to engineer a change in mind-set and to empower young people in Africa to take deliberate action to build the Africa we all crave – an Africa where every citizen prospers!

The next couple of days, Leila, a young talented intern in my team, who had been working with me on this particular project, met with Lucy to dust off the final presentation, do a couple of dry runs and that was it. We knew Lucy was ready. The fact that she was going to deliver a fascinatingly memorable talk was never in doubt. A few weeks after the talk, the organisers reached out to confirm what we had known from the beginning – the talk was great. In their email, they shared the link to the talk with a suggestion: why not call it ***A Bold New Normal***. This was no suggestion. They had named the final talk **A Bold New Normal**.

What followed afterwards, I can only describe as a movement. As the talk generated conversations around the world, we embarked on The Bold New Normal (TBNN) Tour, with young people across many parts of the country and, when Lucy's travelling schedules allowed, a few countries in Africa and Europe. We activated digital campaigns anchored on TBNN and commenced 'Conversations in Boldness' mostly on social media to engage young people all over the continent.

"You need to write a book Lucy", I would re-echo from time to time, the sentiments many had expressed during interactions. To which she would reply, "certainly". It was not lost on her. Lucy has always nurtured the dream of immortalising her thoughts, but I knew too well how stretched her time was. I would often ask her how she seemed to perfectly juggle her various roles – as CEO of a leading multinational telecom business, a full-time and deeply involved mother, a global speaker, STEM Advocate, Coach and Mentor to dozens.

One afternoon in August 2018, a call came through from Lucy. *This must be special*, I thought to myself. Although Lucy and I interacted regularly after we both moved on from the company, it was mostly through WhatsApp messaging and occasional face-to-face meetings. I picked up and the first thing I heard got me totally enthralled.

"I'm writing that book Richard. And I need you to be part of the first meeting with my publishers. Can you make it?"

She had been penning her thoughts silently over the course of several months and was ready to commence the publishing process.

Over the course of the last three years, I have come to know Lucy as a deep thinker and multi-dimensional leader with a burning desire to empower and unleash the potential of people; especially young people. It is at the core of what she does and stands for.

It is this same desire that led her to champion the **Evolve with STEM** initiative to encourage young people to adopt courses in STEM. It is what drove her to initiate national and regional conversations aimed at promoting STEM as an accelerator of Africa's development.

In the golden pages of this bestseller, Lucy channels this desire into a transformational agenda and espouses bold ideas that can only emanate from the mind of a passionate advocate on a mission to inspire, empower and transform.

In *The Bold New Normal*, she draws on her experience, leadership journey and passion to transform Africa's narrative – challenging the curious mind, the doer and the passionate African to take deliberate actions to create the Africa we all desperately crave and need.

The Bold New Normal is more than an idea. It is a movement. It will stretch and challenge your thinking to be more. To do more for yourself, your country, continent and the world at large.

Are you ready for the Bold New Normal Challenge?

Richard Kweku Ahiagble, Communications Consultant & Co-Founder, Upendi PR

INTRODUCTION

"Madam, if you want anything to change you have to get into the gutter with the people" – A young driver delivering a life lesson

When the Caribbean was hit by hurricanes in 2017, news networks across the globe carried the story. The news coverage conveyed compassion for the great loss people were experiencing. I could relate. For one, my mother-in-law is from the Caribbean. Secondly, it had been only a couple of years since torrential rain and subsequent flooding had led to an explosion in Accra that killed almost 200 people on the spot. It was the most horrific scene I had ever seen.

Accra, Ghana's capital, is a low-lying city which opens out to the sea. A growing population and challenged enforcement of urban planning had left the city with waterways that could not deal with the sheer volume of rain. Waterways were now largely inundated with refuse. All this was exacerbated by the growth in the density of people living in the city. To be honest, flooding had become a perennial problem in Accra. That fateful night, the 3rd of June 2015, was one of the most intense experiences for me as a business leader. Parts of the city were under siege. I was fortunate to live close enough to our business office to have made it home long before any of us realised how intense the night would be. I called back to the office to check on people and found out that we had staff stuck in the office. Imagine going to work with a plan to go home at the end of the day, only to realise that you were stuck for the night? I had to make a plan. I got some staff over to my house for the night while others, who preferred to remain in the office, were happy with food supplies. It was the least I could do.

The next day, we found out that we had been the lucky ones. One of the worst hit areas was around the Kwame Nkrumah Circle – named after the first president of Ghana. People had parked their cars at the petrol station. They were waiting for the rain to subside so the roads would become more passable. The ground around them was flooded. It turned out that an underground fuel tank was also flooded, causing fuel to rise to the surface. And, somehow, in the vicinity was an open flame. A spark meets highly flammable fuel. An explosion follows. The station and its environs caught fire. Everything was on fire. Everything.

I pause as I write because the images come flooding back. I only watched on TV and wish I could un-see what I saw. People. People of Ghana. My people. Burnt alive. Using the words 'charred bodies' makes me squeamish. Yet, there they were. Charred in the aftermath of the explosion. Even through the screen, the pain was palpable. How do you comfort a woman who loses her grip on her child only to later realise that her child is gone for good? As you look into her eyes through the screen, you wish there was more that you could do than just empathise.

So, you can understand my intrigue with the Caribbean news reports. I was intrigued that, in the midst of all the pain and loss, the news reports of the Caribbean disaster were also immediately and equally concerned with estimates of how much it would cost to rebuild. *Rebuild!* Yes, this was a natural disaster. Yes, the impact will have to be assessed and lessons learnt. But it all had to be rebuilt! Why didn't I hear this over the June 3rd disaster?

It got me thinking, though. I wondered how many African leaders ever estimate the cost to build our countries. How much would it cost and how long would it take to bring the average African standard of living to the level of the average person in a developed economy? What would it take to do so? Or, better still, do we even recognise the need to build at scale and fully establish African countries? Outcomes, plans, cost, execution and more. More like what policies need to change? Which agreements need to be revisited?

I thought more about whether enough Africans and people of Africa descent globally ever seriously consider what it would take to build their communities to an acceptable average level for the 21st century. Do we even believe our countries deserve to be built? I realise that belief is closely tied to socialisation. I have learnt, through my children, that socialisation plays a significant role in how we see our world and what we expect of it. It plays an even greater role in how we see ourselves and what we believe we are capable of achieving.

Over the years, I have repeated key statements of self-affirmation to my children. My intent has always been for them to understand that my expectations of them are within the realms of their talents, abilities and dreams – competencies that they already possess and many that they will acquire over time. That they are no less than any human being. That they have as valid a part in the future as anyone else.

When they repeat the message, I feel a sense of progress.

"*I know, my mummy always tells me that!*"

Those were the words of my little boy to his nursery teacher. He was about 3 years old. As he got into nursery one morning, she said to him: "You are such a handsome boy". His response was a statement of what he knew to be true of himself; nothing special, just a matter of fact to him. Today, I wonder how many African children hold the same extent of self-confidence as that 3-year-old. Of course, there are some who have been socialised to believe in themselves even more than my children; but have we socialised *enough* of them to hold self-belief dearly?

In November 2016, I was invited to speak at TedxEuston. It was a privilege to find myself invited to this stage and I knew I had to deliver something great. I had 18 minutes to tell the world what was really on my mind. Some ideas had been brewing for a while and I knew this was my opportunity to share them on an international stage.

"2016 will close with a sub-Saharan African population of over one billion. According to the IMF[1], the GDP of this area is 3.1% of global GDP; about the same GDP as Russia with only 144 million people. In 5 years, 3.1% is set to become 3.2%, effectively no change. In 35 years, the world will have 2 billion more people. 1 billion of these will be in sub-Saharan Africa. That means a doubling of the population. That means about half of the sub-Saharan African population will be under 35 years! If today we have inadequate services in healthcare, education and access to jobs, what will happen in 35 years? Today many Africans do not have the opportunity to prosper; prosperity starts with economic opportunity.

"The current trajectory of Africa will not get us where we need to be. We need dramatic inorganic change.

"We need a new normal!"

This is how I started my delivery. I went on…

"I have learnt many lessons on my African journey.

[1]International Monetary Fund

"In 1983, my parents moved my siblings and I to Ghana. Prior to this, I had spent most of my childhood in London. Growing up as a little girl in London, Ghana had come to hold a special place in my mind. I always heard my parents and their friends tell nostalgic stories about Ghana. These stories, coupled with the fact that I thought it was eternally sunny, meant Ghana was only one thing to me: paradise!

"I managed to figure out that there was a small issue of dealing with mosquitoes, but I was sure I could manage that. After all, other people lived there.

"Well, Ghana in 1983 was anything but paradise. It was one of the most difficult years in the country's economic history. The rains had failed and with it crops had failed. Our big neighbour Nigeria decided, partly as payback is what I was to learn later, to expel Ghanaian nationals; one million new mouths arrived in a country that was in the middle of a drought. My family and I were part of the million.

"*Kenkey*[2] is a staple food in southern Ghana. It was so scarce that people were willing to buy it uncooked. *Uncooked* meant an assurance of supply as the buyers would go home and cook it themselves. Wheat flour was also in short supply. Getting hold of bread required relationships with the right people. I was too young to fathom, but I suspected that Ghana must have also been under some kind of sanctions as it was still a country under military rule at the time[3].

"My parents had been gone from Ghana for so long that they did not know any of the supposed right people. They had also both

[2]Kenkey is made from corn dough and cooked in corn or plantain leaves. It serves as a base for many delicious meals.
[3]Ghana held its first democratic elections in 1992 under the Fourth Republic and has been a peaceful democratic nation ever since.

grown up outside the big cities of Accra and Kumasi and only came to work in Accra, where they met, after their education. In those months of hardship, I experienced, first hand, what the majority of the population was going through – a struggle for survival. The harsh reality of insufficient food supplies was stark.

"Thankfully, the rains eventually returned. Farms prospered. Fisher-folk found new supplies and, almost suddenly, there was an abundance of affordable food.

"In retrospect, it means a country like Ghana now has over an entire generation of people for whom the drought of 1983 is at best an old narrative. Thankfully, they live in a country that has steadily made progress. But they, like all young people across the African continent, are not excluded from a narrative of an Africa predominantly characterised by harsh negative images that get more airplay internationally than any other narrative of their achievements. The narrative is behind their times.

"Thankfully, today, countries on the continent know better than to expel each other. And, yes, there are still children on the continent living in survival mode focused on just getting through the day. The question is: *do such children only live in Africa*? Is there a continent in the world that does not have children living in survival mode? And is it reasonable to persist in telling a single version of their African story? Perhaps we need to expand the narrative.

"There is no denying that some of these issues of survival persist. For some, they first have to survive their childhood with limited access to healthcare that will remain the case throughout their lives. If they are fortunate enough, they will get access to education that will provide information but not necessarily challenge them. Fundamentally, this is because most of their education will be based on a narrative that they cannot relate to. An alien narrative. All the while, they will be part of the few more fortunate ones if their parents are able to consistently plan and manage their finances to ensure they do not have to worry about putting food on the table. After all these, they might have the chance to be gainfully employed. What a problem statement! A problem statement of only part of the narrative. A problem statement that is relevant to finding sustainable solutions.

"My experience of this existence early in my childhood, albeit for a relatively short time, never left me. It created a permanent hunger in me to do more and be more; most importantly, to create solutions and be part of those solutions.

"A little over a decade after I arrived, I left Ghana to pursue higher education and to build a career in the UK. I was driven to make the most of every opportunity to develop as an engineer."

Recollecting that opportunity, I wonder about the many young people who today, are willing to risk their very lives to reach Europe in the hope of opportunity. I was fortunate to move across legally. I was also fortunate to have an education that meant that I had access to tertiary instruction even if I had stayed in Ghana. I realise that it is from that vantage point of seeming privilege that I speak.

Yet I cannot help but wonder how it must feel to be willing to risk one's life to get to another land completely unknown, except through the screen of a device or a voice on the radio. Somehow, I do not believe that it is simply material enticements that draw young people across the Mediterranean. Young people who may not know how to swim but are willing to take their chances. Chances that could, and in many instances do, include death.

No. It is not directly about superfluous enticements. It is about the fact that they do not see and realise the opportunities at home. Yes, indeed, their countries are not where they should be developmentally. But, for many of them, they can, if they are willing, build lives that are far better for them right where they are. Lives that will ensure that their personal progress is progress for their nations. That national progress will mean a stronger foundation for future generations.

The real issue is a question of mindset that has been created by a persistent narrative, handed down through generations, via the media, and through formal education that *the enticement of lands unknown* is better. That *what* they come from is worthless. That is the real issue. Mindset!

I continued my talk...

"In 2008, I was fortunate to return to Africa, starting in Ghana, to work in the telecommunications industry. It was an opportunity that allowed me to make the most of my education and experience up to that point. I was a chartered electrical and electronic engineer with a prestigious MBA. Among my many hopes and dreams, I came along with my hunger to desperately influence change on the continent. I felt my intentions were well-placed so why were most of those early days filled with frustration? Nothing was right in my eyes. There was so much opportunity to complain. Not enough order, not enough timeliness, not enough speed.

"Sometimes we think our presence alone is enough. I suspect I thought so too. Presence is not enough. It is not enough to show up expecting that we have some superior way of thinking about solutions and not realise that we lack the contextual reference points to be relevant. It contributes to the lack of sustainability of imported solutions. Solutions that seem great elsewhere but act as a bandage at best when imported into African countries".

I needed to figure this out for myself. Why was the romance of my new-found purpose draining from my heart? I set about trying to understand the context and people. A context I had never worked in as an adult. I needed to talk to more of the people for whom I thought change mattered the most. One such conversation has stayed with me.

I was talking to a driver in our company about change and he said *"Madam, if you want anything to change, you have to get into the gutter with the people"*.

For all my years of education and experience, he had probably taught me the biggest leadership lesson about changing outcomes for people.

It is the sort of change that we must lead from the *inside out*, not from the *outside in*. What he meant was that I have to walk in peoples' shoes to influence lasting change and I believe all of us who want to see a great Africa will need to do so. His words also meant that it is the people who live and breathe the African experience that can best solve Africa's problems. The best solutions must come from the hearts and hands that live the African experience.

Change is happening where the people of the continent are choosing change. Their actions create inspiration for others.

"In 2010, my company promoted me to a bigger role in its operations in the Democratic Republic of Congo (DRC). This was not a straightforward move, but it turned out to be transformational to my career".

Recalling my move to the DRC brings to mind the story of a marketing consultant who came to work with us as a group of national companies. The sessions were organised to have representation from all our operations across the continent. She had done a tour of some of the countries and had concluded that "they are all the same"!

Familiar thinking. Needless to say, she was not African. Many people outside Africa refuse to see the diversity of Africa. But for a supposed expert, I was taken aback by how flippantly she dismissed the various countries as 'the same'. I have taken my time to analyse sameness from her perspective. Why would she assume all countries are the same? I came to the conclusion that, perhaps, her perspective was influenced by the developmental gulf between her country and countries in Africa. That, to her, the differences between countries on this diverse continent was marginal compared to the difference between her country and all those she had visited on the continent. I like to think that she was making an objective business consideration from *her* point of view. Her consideration of immateriality had left me surprised; yet given me real food for thought. It was eye-opening to take the time to reflect on and attempt to understand what the continent looks like from the outside in.

Although, to some people Africa seems all the same, for many people within Africa the differences between the various countries are real. The differences predate modern history, centuries before colonisation and independence, all the way down to present economic performance; not to mention subtleties of language and culture. Even just listening to my parents, who are from different parts of Ghana, I hear of people who have taken different paths to get to where they are today. How then can one reduce this complex narrative to simply *same*?

But I digress. I was talking about moving to the DRC.

"Many well-wishers discouraged this move, yet I embraced it. I embraced the opportunity it presented to not just me but to my family. A chance to explore and discover another African country. A chance to embrace a rich culture. A chance to encounter new languages. I consciously focused on the goodness of the move. There is goodness everywhere, if we choose to find it."

As part of the change journey we are on, we must figure out how to focus on positive commonalities, embrace differences positively and work together.

I became the Chief Marketing Officer of my company in the DRC. While there, I met an inspired young man. This inspired young man worked in IT security in my company and he made a simple request. He asked to join the marketing team to run a new product category called *data*. This encompassed all things internet as we knew it back then. So, we came to an agreement that, for a period, he would do both jobs – sustaining one and learning the other.

"Jean-Claude's performance was so exceptional that we saw exponential growth in the data revenue stream. His career success has seen him go on to work in Senegal, Ghana and other locations. He has mentored many young African professionals along the way. He is arguably one of the best assets the continent has in facing the digital future. And today he is in the process of creating one such company".

People need leadership that will inspire them to greater ambition and also create opportunities for them to realise their potential. The leadership must be visible and set the right tone and example of focus, hard work, dedication, integrity and consistency. I suspect that this is what many of the young people risking their lives across the Mediterranean are seeking.

Africa taught me to lead. Has Africa taught herself to lead?

I get emotional when I reflect on my leadership journey. Africa taught me to be a great leader because my pivotal years of leadership development were all experienced in Africa. I learnt to survive in Africa, I learnt to lead effectively by walking in people's shoes in Africa and I have inspired others to lead in Africa. But Africa has not taught herself these lessons well enough.

Over two decades have passed since I graduated from my 'survival class' and Africa is still surviving. In fact, surviving remains the norm for many on the continent and this is not acceptable. It is not acceptable for a continent blessed with the greatest human capital and unrivalled natural resources. It is unacceptable for a continent whose citizens have built nations around the world to continue to survive. How is it possible that the Democratic Republic of Congo alone has the largest reserves of the Coltan used in electronic devices around the world and yet remains poor? There is no country supplier of a global good that is poor except in Africa. This poverty can only be defined as structural. Globally structural! It is the product of systemic sustained disadvantage constructed to sustain the interests of a few on the continent and many outside the continent. It is structured to provide for the excess of a few and the expense of many in our world.

Eradicating poverty seems to be a repetitive goal. A repetitive goal that never seems to be attained. This is simply too small a vision for Africa. No other continent in the world developed by setting an ambition purely to eradicate poverty. We need a new vision that says we no longer eliminate the problem, but we create lasting solutions. We must no longer survive life in Africa, we must thrive in Africa.

But when a region *seems* so far behind what do we do to close the gap?

I love running. Admittedly I am a poor sprinter; those genes were reserved for my son. I preferred endurance running when I had the muscle for it. But picture the scene. Imagine running a 100-metre race. Do you focus on getting away from the starting line or on being the first to reach the finish line? These two visions of success in the race are not the same. If the goal is to get away from the start line, then one step is all it takes to succeed. However, to get to the finish line one has to persist and endure the strain to finish the race. Eradicating poverty is like focusing on getting away from the start! It is simply a bar too low.

As if reaching the finish line is not enough of a challenge, the real scenario is worse. An even clearer picture is a race where I am at the start line of a race with Usain Bolt. However, Usain has been given a 50-metre head start! My task is to at least catch up with Usain. We can all agree that my chances of success are nil unless Usain stops running or, somehow, I develop muscles and techniques that exceed his.

That is the story of developmental progress playing out. In this scenario I represent an establishing nation in Africa, while Usain represents a developed country I am supposedly catching up with. Given what we know, without rethinking the race and some form of accelerating technology allowed in the race to give me a boost, I have absolutely no chance. No chance at all of closing the gap.

In other words...

In a village without water, is building a borehole the end game or an interim step toward a reliable automated water supply system which will not only improve health but the economic fortunes of the village? Is the borehole a strategic solution or an interim tactic? Why do we persist in seeing the borehole as an end in itself? Why end at the applause for a borehole? It is simply not enough!

It is not enough to build roads to connect the rural to the urban. It is not enough to bring in investors. It is not enough to provide some form of education and healthcare. It is just not enough to provide a solution for today. The vision must be bigger, it must capture the long term, and it must consider the benefits for generations to come.

We are not working to be less poor. That is what eradication of poverty is about and it is simply inadequate. If our goal is purely the eradication of poverty, then we need to refocus. We must work for the people of the continent to prosper. By prosperity I mean an Africa where decent healthcare, education, shelter and food are assured. An Africa where a young person can realistically expect to find gainful employment.

Africa needs a new normal. We agree on the need to raise and mentor great leaders. But we need greater ambition. We also need to agree on what acceleration looks like. We need to inspire and create opportunities of innovation and creativity built on a much bigger vision. When you are running behind in a race, you must realise your need to run faster than the people ahead of you just to stop falling behind. Stop falling behind and start closing the gap. Then keep up. Being satisfied with small incremental progress is not enough.

We need a **bold Africa where the basics of life are assured so people flourish by self-actualisation like anyone else on the planet.** We need an Africa where we believe the rights of the African are truly equal to the rights of anyone else on the planet.

We need to rise boldly to prosper!

Now back to the 3.1%...

3.1% is close to Russia's contribution to global GDP of 3.3% in 2015. 3.1% was actually sub-Saharan Africa's share of GDP in 2015. And unlike Russia's 144 million population, this represents the livelihoods of the 1 billion people who live in sub-Saharan Africa. 3.1% is supporting 14% of the world's population.

That does not count as rising; that is *surviving*...

We must create a different Africa. The Africa where everyone has the chance to prosper.

So here is my humble request. The next time someone tells you about Africa rising tell them it is not enough. Because in 2021 that GDP figure is set to rise to a 'whopping' 3.2% with a population of 1.1 billion in sub-Saharan Africa.

An annual growth rate of even 10% is not enough to close the gap quickly enough. Starting from a low base means that Africa needs aggressive growth rates. However, economists will make it abundantly clear that it is a structurally unrealistic rate. What we need is sustained high growth rates. Sustained over decades. Which is why we have to talk about another way from the current way. A way that changes our normal and reorients us.

Let us rather talk about the bold new normal.

Our bold new normal is to create the Africa where everyone prospers.

It is a matter of vision, choice and action.

We need a new mindset.

To change mindsets we need a new language. A language that speaks of success.

To change our language – what we profess – we need a new vision. We need to agree on visions of what successful outcomes for Africa look like.

We must be the generation that creates a new Africa that will one day be the great history our children read about.
So please join me on this new journey.

A journey of discovery.
A journey of creation.
A journey of high productivity.
A journey of realising potential.
A journey of the manifestation of the true Africa.

This is not only a call to Africans.

While I was at business school, I was the President of the Africa Club. I made one important call. The club was for anyone who identified with Africa for whatever positive reason – descent, business, humanitarian etc. – and with this book I am making that same call again. It is a book for anyone who identifies with Africa and believes that true development is possible.

This book is a call to everyone to define and execute a bold new normal for societies who identify with the realities of Africa around the world. While it is about African descent it is not only about Africans. Just like we join hands to address issues affecting various disadvantaged groups around the world it will take collective global effort and will to turn the fortunes of African people around. Of course, Africans themselves must lead the change but sustainable change will only come through collective effort.

Why? Because the current state of Africa is a product of a collective deliberate global design. A deliberate imbalanced design. Together we can redesign Africa.

Are you in? My hope is that this book will inspire you to challenge the structural imagined reality of Africa and take new actions that create a new path to continental prosperity.

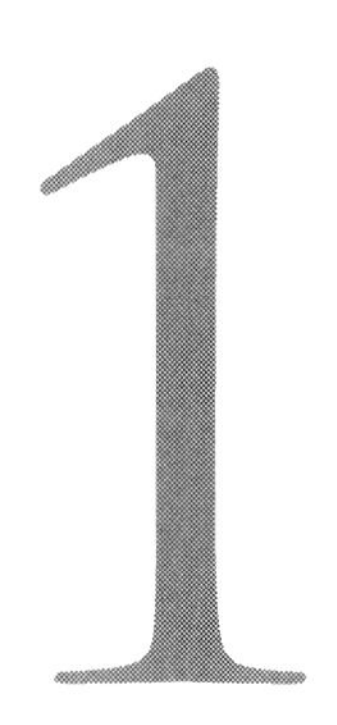

'...one of the most mis-managed brands in history.'

AFRICA!

"Why is 'Africa' predominantly used as a diminutive description?"

Now I have to be honest, I don't like the use of the word 'Africa'. I believe it is an over-generalisation of a complex continent – 54 countries and over 1 billion people. I also don't like using it because it is seen more for what is missing rather than for what there is. Personally, the word 'Africa' represents a land of potential prosperity that I pray its own people will discover.

When I was in Business school, I loved my early exploration into marketing communication. I got along with many of my professors, including Erin Andersen, of blessed memory. A sad loss indeed. I went up to her one day and said "Erin, I love marketing. However, my plan is to go and work somewhere in Africa one day. I don't think marketing is entirely relevant". Her response was straight to the point. Africa desperately needed marketing. It needed people like me to rebrand and market what has been one of the most mis-managed brands in history. Over subsequent encounters she would share with me lessons from marketing management in the USA. She opened my mind to the possibility of a new African image.

Over the years of working on the continent, her words have consistently rung true. How much of Africa's narrative is truly based on fact?

I heard a lion bark. Sounds ridiculous, right? Lions don't bark, they roar.

So why do we believe everything we read and hear about Africa even when it is from sources who have never set foot on the continent? How can someone who has never seen the continent be a credible reference point? Why must the expert so frequently be the person who does not know the continent? We cannot treat an entire continent as the external to be studied relative to a reality outside itself.

With my writing, I am reaching out particularly to young people in Africa with a simple request: question what you see and hear. Sadly, I have encountered numerous people who express subjective opinions that are unsubstantiated. These opinions soon become unverified facts that are repeated. Yet as these facts are repeated, what purpose does the narrative serve you?

And more often than not they are negative about our potential and our future. So many debates are about doom and gloom. Frequent debates on the depreciation and appreciation of African currencies, the dependence on commodities, corruption…the negative branding, the list goes on. I do not know everything about everything, so I ask those who know to explain to me. When I know more, I can make informed decisions. Shouldn't we all? Should we not commit to verifying what we hear not only to learn but to be part of the solution?

Perhaps the most persistent negative branding of Africa is on leadership. The assumption that Africa is bereft of leaders impacts Africa's image more than anything else – for a people without leadership are lost. So, sustaining the negative narrative, rather than identifying good leadership, leaves our young people feeling parentless in the proverbial sense. It is a narrative that young people repeat and imbibe negativity of their own selves.

We cannot be negative speculators. We must build our future on facts – a solid foundation for sustained development.

We must think positively about each country in Africa knowing that we have all we need to create great nations. Don't fan the flames of negativity – the glass is half full, not half empty! Let's make the most of it starting with a positive attitude towards what works.

The Africa I See

So, if we are to be positive, what does Africa mean to you?

What it means to me is a place where the population will more than double in a generation!

For the majority of people reading this, it is within our lifetime. In that time, our children will be the adults running the continent.

What issues will they contend with? Are we laying a strong enough foundation to give them a chance of success?

If today, we think healthcare, education and economic opportunity are inadequate, how are we going to cope in 2050?

That same Africa means opportunity. The land where all the things that need to be fixed present opportunities for the African to prosper. Africa will continue to have an enormous wealth of human capital to nurture and realise their potential.

Africa to me means a place where we must do all we can today, to ensure that the future we all know is possible is brought to life for Africans.

But first we must contend with the issue of bias.

One form of bias presupposes that what a person is capable of is based on their physical and circumstantial attributes. Our most obvious physical attribute is our seeming race and ethnicity. The greatest bias against Africans realising their potential is created by the subliminal messages people receive over time. We cannot deny the fact that the definition and expectations of Africa are still a result of centuries-old perceptions of Africa. The sorts of ideas documented many years ago. Captured in history books and scientific journals. Journals obsessed with human classification and the creation of narratives that justify exclusion. History books that tell stories from an external point of view. A view that is founded on the discovery of people who are different. These messages have created a sustained negative bias that, in many cases, are held by Africans themselves. These narratives are taught in schools to generation after generation with many now believing their own history started on the arbitrary date of independence declaration.

Think of the fact that shock and surprise still persist when an extraordinary human feat is attained by someone of Africa descent. They are deemed to be the lucky ones who made it, they are told. Bias does not always emanate from ill-intention. More often than not, it is from misconception and ignorance. Accepted untruths that hardly evolve.

So, we must deliberately redress misconceptions. It would be easy to cheer people on and say, "let bias build strength in you!" But that is an outlier's game. Outliers exist in every society, but they don't represent the average person. For the average person, it is exhausting to have to constantly deal with bias, to say the least.

The biggest persistent communication campaign on Africa is the communication shared by aid and charitable agencies. This tune has not substantially changed in my lifetime. It is the standard narrative of a destitute African child, desperate for your pocket change to survive. That needs to change. It is the greatest source of bias; for if a person is bombarded with these images, how can this African child possibly be equal to other children on other continents?

For most people, Africa is nothing more than a place where starving children need to be saved.

We must challenge and stop this deeply negative branding.

Now, I appreciate that this is a polarising topic, but it has to be discussed. So here is my submission.

All over the world, there are people who need a safety net. A tactical solution to a present economic challenge. And, yes, many of those people reside in Africa – a populous continent. But why do so many reside on one continent despite being thousands of miles apart in different countries? What are the historical factors that have created this geographical gap and continental cluster?

We cannot change history but is charity the most effective lever for progress? And if it is, why hasn't it worked so far? If you believe it has worked, then please do share facts on sustainability.

I submit that we must stop undermining the humanity of the African with degrading communication and rather re-engage on sustainable economic terms. We must lead the way in ensuring that every African child discovers their worth and engages the world on an even keel.

At this point the conversation typically veers towards "Ah, but it is their leaders". The easy excuse. I recall a case study shared on the internet. The title went something like: 'Lessons in bad leadership from Africa'. Essentially, an all-encompassing how not to lead – Africa special – written by a non-African! I, like many others, protested. The story was taken down. Over 1 billion people, 54 countries, 54 heads of state and many leaders in business, economic, social and religious life. The author could have chosen, for that one article on Africa, to write about the best of leadership in challenging circumstances. But, no, the punch bag needed another punch.

Let's stop allowing people the leadership excuse. It is an excuse for the African who does not want to change but rather apportion blame. It is an excuse that provides the non-African with justification for disingenuous engagement with the continent. It is an excuse that objectifies the powerless African by taking away their rights because it is all down to *their* bad leaders.

What we focus on grows. What if we decided to focus on what is great about African leadership? What if we treated Africa as a source of worthy lessons? Will our focus on greatness create more greatness?

I personally know how liberating it is to refuse to live a life boxed by other people's bias. But not everyone is fortunate enough to be socialised in that way. And so, we should and must change our bias towards Africa.

Perhaps, it is the last frontier of bias.

It still remains one to be addressed.

2

"African countries must stop begging for everything from foreigners" – Kofi Annan (UN Secretary-General, 1997-2006)

WHICH AFRICA?

I could not agree more with the late Kofi Annan. African countries must all learn their worth. They must engage their world and ensure real value is placed on their contributions.

Perception matters!

Africa needs rebranding. Rebranding not just as a continent but actually each country needs to be rebranded. Rebranded authentically. Rebranded not just in words but in deeds that act on the words.

We need the people of Africa to believe in a different brand identity for their countries. A brand identity that speaks of the best of their country today and the future they want to create.

Some countries are already on that journey. Rwanda comes to mind. When I hear people critical of the country's progress, I always wonder how those critics would have coped in 1994 and the years leading up to the horrific events. Having visited the country several times, I am clear what rebranding a country, first for its own citizens, is really like. An inclusive rebranding that the people buy into may not be perfect, but it beats many other examples. The country is on a change journey across generations that requires persistence. Persistence not only in action but to deal with missteps. Can you imagine how other countries on the continent could build on this identity? How businesses could build on that identity?

There are many other suggestions on rebranding. Yet another example, David Ofosu-Dorte's view of Ghana, is of the only country that exists closest to the centre of the world. Literally the centre chosen centuries ago and even more relevant to us today. *Ghana, the centre of the world.*

Not everyone likes the idea of a changed image of African countries. In 2018, I remember the shock of reporting around the world that followed Ghana's president's 'Ghana Beyond Aid' speech. Nana Addo-Dankwa Akufo-Addo was with France's Emmanuel Macron and the world could not believe that he would set such a tone. To many, the idea was too ambitious. Many, over subsequent months, went on to prove how this was not possible. They gave all the reasons why it would not work. It was simply not possible for an African country to thrive to the point of not needing aid!

What a wrong focus! Young Ghanaians and Africans need to know it is possible, because their leaders told them so: to *live beyond aid*. It will take the sweat off their own brows. It will take them valuing what they have. It will take them holding themselves and others to account. But, most importantly, they have to believe that it is possible. That is what bold visions are about!

To criticise bold ambition is to say we do not actually believe in the possibility of self-actualisation for the African. I take a different approach. One that says a brighter future is possible.

If you could choose a new identity for your country what would it be? Why would you choose this identity? What would it mean for your country?

It is time to rebuild Africa's image to project its people, their capacity, ability and enormous contribution to global economics! The current distorted impression needs to evolve.

Leadership must look beyond what is seen to what is possible. The question should be, *what should I do to make these visions come true?* Doubting means a perpetual commitment to hardship. We must change our created reality.

On one of my many business trips, I was struck by two experiences in the same location. I was in Dubai.

As a waitress served me, she asked where I lived. I said "Ghana" and she asked where that was. So, I described where to find Ghana in West Africa. Her immediate response to that was "Oh Africa! I would love to go there one day for a safari!"

I did not have the heart to tell her that Ghana has no wild lions! That her safari to game parks was possible but not in the way she imagines. I suppose, to her, Africa is all the same place. Regardless of which country I mentioned, it would have been all the same. And for that matter there must be a safari! What a limited and limiting view.

In another instance, as a colleague put up a projection of Africa to discuss business, the outline of the continent was filled with images of vegetation and animals. How were they relevant to the business discussion? Why are these the first things that come to mind when business is run by and for people? How can a business discussion bypass the fact that there are over a billion people on the continent and characterise a continent in this way?

Africa is the only continent where the animals and natural resources are thought of before the people. Africa is the only continent where what the inhabitants offer is underplayed. Africa is the only continent where *what you are supposed to be* is more important than *what you could become*.

Development is built on human capacity; our ability to dream and the new outcomes we create by realising our potential. Africa has great entrepreneurs, scientists, performers and leaders in various fields. We have pioneers. Of course, there is more work to do but where in the world is there no work to be done? Why do we continue to allow people to think of wide-open plains as Africa and ignore the thriving cities? Why does the narrative continue to centre on what is missing rather than what is positively evolving?

Rebranding Africa starts with its own brand ambassadors. All Africans, home or away, must remember that they are representatives of Africa's narrative. Each of us must consciously ask himself or herself: *which story will I leave behind*?

Few people share the story of what it is truly like to live the Africa Experience. Fewer still hear the story told.

The hardest part is that the stories that get heard are usually those told by people who do not live the Africa Experience. They are told as a perspective from a vantage point looking in. A vantage point of a helicopter view passed on to them without ever stepping foot on the continent.

I am thankful for some parts of the story that are told. Today, stories abound on the creation of new technologies by young Africans. I see fashion being communicated differently. These stories abound but still exist on a small scale. A scale too small to drown out the negative narrative. We can tell richer stories if we tell the story through the hearts and eyes that live it on global platforms.

We need to be ambassadors first to each other and, then, to the world. To recount the whole story we live. How we are changing a continent. How we are blazing a trail that is uniquely ours. How the Africa of the history books is fading.

We need to bring to the world an updated view of Africa.

I applaud all the people, especially young, who I see projecting truer, more balanced, images of Africa. A lot of potential is being realised and this is what must be top of mind for Africa!

If we don't support young people in valuing what they have, they will inevitably lose it. A man once sold his birthright for a meal. He thought nothing of it until years later when it was time to claim his birthright. He could not believe it was gone. He thought 'how dare you!' Realising our potential requires that we place value on our birthright. I speak of the biblical parable of Esau and Jacob. Esau sold his birthright to his brother for short term satisfaction – a simple meal. Regardless of what you make of this simple story, the lesson of valuing what we have in our hands must not be lost. It is one of those stories that rings true across many facets of life on the African continent.

When I was in the Democratic Republic of Congo, I worked with an amazing young woman. I loved having lunch with my team; that is when I learnt many of the lessons that would give me a wider perspective on the realities of life as we shared and discussed experiences, both personal and from people we knew. Over lunch one day, this brilliant young woman said to me: "Lucy, the problem with many parts of Africa is that people make decisions with their stomachs".

A profound statement from a woman in her 20s that has stayed with me. What she meant was that, all too often, we sacrifice long-term sustainable gain for a short-term hit. We exchange what is our birthright – that should sustain our countries for generations – for short-term benefits that satisfy immediate hunger. The price is typically high in the long run. Africa has been the storehouse of resources to the world for centuries. How is it that the long-term benefit of this wealth mainly benefits countries outside the continent?

Short term thinking! That is the way of people living with a mentality based on survival. It would be easy to point towards a particular group of individuals and blame them for this. Too easy to say it is about this leader and that individual who is good for nothing. Way too easy.

But that is not the challenge. The question is, *faced with the same choices what would you and I do differently*?

Would it be our stomach that makes the decision or our head, influenced by our long-term vision? Would we live with today's hunger to the benefit of tomorrow's wealth? Would we let the charms of what we can get for what we have today undermine our ability to act and invest in the future of those to come? And yet part of the change required is for us to understand the African experience. Understanding the experience will help us understand what leads to behaviour like this.

Change is tough. Especially when it is about a large number of people. The people leading the change have one thing in common – courage! Courage sets them apart! We need to be extremely courageous and build on our ideas for the continent.

This may sound simple, but we live in a world where it takes courage to accept that we are equally made in the image of the Creator. That all of how we present externally is valid in a beautifully diverse world.

There are times when courage is required for the simplest things too.

I found myself needing to tap in to courage for what seemed like the strangest of reasons. The 6th of August 2016 marked a day of courage for me. I went to see my hairdresser and asked her to give me a short haircut. The shortest of my adult life as it left me with about an inch and a half of kinky curly hair.

At this point you are probably wondering why I am talking about hair as inspiration for courage. You have to be me on the day to know how I felt. How I felt as a conditioned person.

I talk about hair because of conditioning. Conditioning that requires courage to overcome. I was surprised at how I reacted post this simple process of getting a haircut. It took courage to do it in the first place – I have only ever done this as a school girl. As school girls in Ghana, we were required to wear our hair short. We wore hair that we scarcely embraced. One of our major post school goals was to straighten our hair as quickly as possible.

So, on the 6th of August, my reaction was mixed; feeling a sense of release, yet wondering *Is this ok? Is it ok for a senior executive woman to step out looking like this?*

It sounds so final. As though my look on the day would characterise my image for the rest of time. Yet that is how many young people are left feeling. They feel that acknowledging and highlighting their authenticity is not good enough. Their version of authentic is somehow subpar, inferior if you may. It certainly should not require courage. It should simply be a matter of course. My hair grew out and sometimes I miss my much shorter hair. Looking back at an image from the day, I looked visibly petrified. Today I can laugh at myself. Yet I still wonder how many young African women are left feeling inadequate and, in some cases, petrified because of their appearance. Why should they feel inferior to others?

It took that act for me to finally complete the full cycle of self-acceptance. I, a confident, progressive and forward-thinking woman needed this act. Today, I fully embrace all of me, including my wonderful hair texture and I look forward to revisiting a short crop in future.

The simplicity of this short story is lost on many people. Yet, I have since wondered why we were all desperate to have our hair chemically altered to straight the moment we left school. And if not straight, why are we at pains to cover it with hair substitutes that do not resemble our own? It says something about how we feel about our image as young women. Our fears and cheers are clearly expressed in our hair. Why must we be afraid to present ourselves to the world as we are? Why is the fear of being the *other* so deep-seated? We should not underestimate the narrative of other. This other that is spoken of is about an association with inferiority. A negative complex that runs deep for many and needs to be deliberately addressed.

Instead of suppression, let's engender courage in our young people by first creating acceptance of self.

I have yet another hair memory. It was circa 2008/2009. I was on a business trip to Sierra Leone with my colleagues who were all non-African. As we stood waiting for a speedboat to get across to the airport, I saw a group of school girls staring at me from across the road. I caught their gaze. I wondered why they stared at me so much. I may have looked wrongly placed but I doubt it was that simple. I think it was more about the mirror they were looking into which made me again think about my hair. My long artificial hair running down my face, to be precise. In that moment, I felt I had let them down. I felt a sense of betraying them. I felt I was presenting them with a future image of a professional woman that would mean them changing themselves to become her.

I know this because, growing up, I felt this – many times. I now embrace the diversity of styling that is available but refuse to accept that the authentic look of an African woman is not an option. Why must we embrace every image and not include our own in the beautiful repertoire?

As you read, I hope that you are building your own courage. Challenge yourself to something positively daring. Something that scares you a little but could open up a new world to you.

Something that makes you ask yourself "Is it ok for ME to go this far?"

After all, the great visions we have are of things that don't exist. Courage is part of the journey to realise them.

Our dreams must certainly include economic progress. For people to thrive, they must move from poverty to prosperity. It is the way it has played out all over the world.

In our journey to prosperity, the people affected must be directly involved; not only in the creation of solutions but the delivery of the solutions.

Each year the 'International Day for the Eradication of Poverty' is celebrated. I am compelled to reflect on what it will take to truly lift people out of poverty.

What kind of systemic change will it take for us to celebrate the creation of prosperity and not the eradication of poverty? What is the right focus for us to truly prosper?

As a business leader, when I set ambitious goals, I don't let where the business is today dictate where it will be in future. Rather, I decide what the future should look like and plan what needs to be done to get there. I focus on the finish line and keep my efforts on getting there rather than focusing on getting away from where I am today.

I believe the same applies if we want to eradicate poverty – our focus should be on devising what our prosperous future looks like together and working tirelessly to get there. Regardless of where we are today. It is about asking *what do we need to do to prosper,* rather than *what do we need to do to stop being poor*. A different point of view, but a very significant shift in viewpoints.

So, let's go ahead and do some redefinition.

Africa is a continent of prosperity!

Africa and her people are blessed with prosperity. It is a continent that represents one of the largest people groups on the planet. Collectively, its people represent the highest population base – 1.2 billion on the continent, at least 0.3 billion in the Americas and more in other locations. The slave trade alone transported 12.5 million people out of Africa over four hundred years. Four hundred years during which their labour built the foundation of every industry as we know it today. Their labour, and absence from their own continent, provided the manpower to create institutionalised wealth that determines global wealth distribution to this day.

Indeed, Africa's people and resources have contributed the most to the wealth of other nations – largely for free.

Today, Africa boasts of the world's largest burgeoning youth population, still the most natural resources and, contrary to what is reported, most of its citizens live in peace as far as their day-to-day lives are concerned. It is rather strange that the continent that was subdued, because its people lived peacefully enough not to mass-produce weapons, should be branded as being war-torn. It is even more ironic that nations who mass produce, sell, distribute and use weapons to control others should be branded as peaceful.

Africa's branding – and the branding of black slaves for that matter – is to systemically justify the treatment of the African as less than. Most of what is perceived of Africa, even by Africans, is deliberately skewed to present the continent as less than. It conveniently justifies Africa's structured disadvantages while no one outside of Africa has to acknowledge the benefits gained.

I bet at this point you are wondering to yourself: *if it is so great, why do we have the challenges Africans and the rest of the world continue to talk about?*

Simple: mindset!

There is a widely-known saying that "the hardest thing to open is a closed mind". Will you open your mind to change?

Africa has all the ingredients needed for its people to experience its prosperity. But that experience will only happen if we open our minds to it. We must create new visions of Africa in our minds. We must let these visions inspire the language we use to speak of positive outcomes for Africa. Our words will change mindsets and open them up. With open minds we will do the work on the ground to make change.

And, particularly for young people, I encourage you to build businesses and careers that create African prosperity. Look beyond yourself and personal needs to the possibility of being one of the creators of the new Africa.

I am not saying the road will be easy. I am saying keep your eye on the prize!

3

Who is Africa?

'Why isn't all of how I was made good enough?'

"What is her true identity? What is her brand?

Whether you try to or not, you will have a brand. Question is, *what will it be*?

Particularly in Africa, this is a relevant question. We need to deliberately create and communicate our brands more effectively.

In 2015, I had the opportunity to share my thoughts on branding with an audience at the CIMG[4].

[4]Chartered Institute of Marketing, Ghana

Even though I was speaking in the context of business, these points are relevant for our African brand. A few points:

1. What is Africa's place in the world? What is the vision? What is the essence of Africa's brand?
2. We need to make the vision of Africa plain and clear, so that all our people can buy into it. Our people are the first and true ambassadors. Ambassadors first to each other, before anyone else.
3. We must deliberately live our brand essence, so others can also feel and connect with us.
4. We must manage our communication and presence. We must own our messaging.
5. We must persist and be consistent to build lasting change of what we are known for.

Doing all of that takes courage.

I can imagine that, like me, you have had many experiences that required courage you never knew you had. It is a feat to allow your courage to take you to new heights; beyond where just your skills can take you.

How willing are you to grow your courage? Can you challenge yourself to something positively daring? It is time to step out of the 'minority' shadow and own our majority!

After all, the great visions we have are of things that don't exist. Courage is part of the journey to realise them.

As I recounted early on, I cut my hair in August 2016, reverting it to its natural form. It was the third time in my adult post-school life that I had done this.

The first time that happened I was a young mother. I had had my first child and took the precautions, I thought, to ensure no chemical treatment harmed my unborn baby. I carried on with it as I went on to study for my MBA with my new baby. My hair was the last thing I had time for. And yet, at the end of my studies, as I searched for a new job, I reverted to my old chemically-treated style as I thought this was essential to my success.

A few years later, as I became the mother of yet another child, I went through the same process. This time, I kept my hair going in its natural state for years as I focused on developing a new phase of my career with young children. Hair did not feature in my list of priorities.

This third time in 2016 was, however, different. I had been contemplating a change again when my little girl started demonstrating a dislike of her own hair. It was 2015 and she was 10. She kept asking when she could have chemically treated hair – like mine. I realised that I had set a standard for her that meant her aspiration was different from what she saw in the mirror.

Isn't that how most African girls, and boys, grow up now? Thinking that all of how each of them was made is not good enough? That, to succeed, self must change?

Don't get me wrong. I appreciate the diversity of style, including hair, which we live. I am sure I will continue to participate in this diversity. But the question I asked myself was simply this: *why isn't all of how I was made good enough? Why can't I show up just as I was made? Why can't my natural hair be one style of the many possibilities?*

I knew I had work to do. The truth is that most of us have lost the art of beautifying what we were given. I set about on a journey of self-education. An education of how to take care of my hair. To make the most of it and embrace it as it is before attempting to understand that which is from elsewhere. YouTube proved to be a wonderful resource for my re-education.

Africans are more than our bodies. Our bodies are the shells that house us. They house us with all our wonderful talents, abilities, hopes and dreams. The way we look does not make these talents, abilities, hopes and dreams any less valid. And, yet, our dissatisfaction with the shell undermines our ability to be all that we can be.

So, let's remind that little girl and little boy that they are indeed, fearfully and wonderfully made just as they are. That their shell is no different from any shell around the world. That they should look beyond their shells to realise the potential that lies within.

After all, they are worth more than their shells!

So, I ask again, "Who is Africa?" The closest there is to a collective called Africa is the African Union. But how representative is that? How does a union truly represent the diversity of Africa?

In the summer of 2018, I was in a taxi in the UK. As we drove along the driver focused on the radio. I was busy on my phone. The discussion seemed to get the better of him. It was a discussion justifying the need for the Gulf Wars – or so it sounded to me. The driver, who appeared to be Asian, turned to me and asked whether I was listening. As I had caught bits of the conversation I politely said "yes". He complained and said to me how unfair it was that the caller to the show assumed the wars were justified. He started to explain his views to me and then turned it over to me. He said to me "You know what it is like. You had Mandela and apartheid. He was in jail for 26 or 27 or 25 years and he stood up for his people". I nodded politely. I did not have the heart to explain to him how equally narrow his view was. I am not from South Africa, so I cannot claim to have personally experienced apartheid.

A short conversation that demonstrates how we have come to assume so much when in reality we know so little. I assumed he was 'Asian'. He assumed I was 'African'. Stereotypes got the better of the conversation. We never sought to understand the specifics of each other and were having a conversation about a caller to a radio station, probably European, who was sharing one aspect of his views. Standing in our individual corners, I am convinced that we each got some aspects wrong. But, in general, uninformed views of Africa and Africans are assumed to be, by definition, right.

So, what does the African Union mean to anyone when it is about so many countries who don't fully recognise each other?

I have spent a lot of time reflecting on this question. It is not enough to remember the existence of the union. We must ask ourselves: *to what end?*

Ghana is a proud founding nation of the AU. I am inspired by the vision of the leaders who continue to drive the AU. Yet we need a more effective AU. One that believes in, and delivers on, the potential of each African. To do so, we need each African nation to harness the potential of its people. We need each African to play their part.

It is a message I shared with a group of secondary school children. It was in 2016 at a school in Mataheko, a suburb of Accra in Ghana. Here is what I told them:

> *Your physical shell has nothing to do with your mental capacity. None of us are spectators. None of us are here for the ride. When we move, Ghana moves. We are Ghana. Have a new vision of what is possible. Let what you say tie into the vision you have. Once your vision informs what you say, you will change your mindset. The first person you need to lead is yourself. To develop our country, we need people like you to be bold.*

So, each must work, each in their sphere of influence, to make countries great. Great countries work better together. Only then will the AU be truly great.

Sometimes when I have these conversations some people promptly ask about the role of tradition in each country's development. The question often comes with an air of denigrating tradition to mean a proxy for backwardness. I believe tradition is relevant. It is relevant because it holds truths that may be communicated differently but resound in their countries and beyond. Here's a story.

Once upon a time, there was a woman who lived in southern Ghana. This woman was fortunate to be the oldest child of a prosperous chief and farmer. She spent her entire life nurturing her extended family. She had 9 children, only 3 survived into adulthood. But, in the period she lived in, losing children was seen as normal.

Overtime, this woman, who had never stepped foot in a classroom, developed the ability to diagnose and treat most ailments that her family members suffered.

One of her many chores was fetching water from her village stream. This stream had the clearest filtered water you could imagine. She had a very special relationship with the stream. She would literally talk to the stream when she went to fetch a bucket of water. She would carefully clear the stream of weeds and anything else that would obstruct flow. She allowed that stream to thrive. Only her youngest child was formally educated. All her grandchildren, on the other hand, were formally educated. How does one translate what is known traditionally in one language to young people educated in a completely different language? The answer is that it is virtually impossible. The undocumented science of healing this woman knew was completely lost on her grandchildren.

Quite frankly, as I watched my grandmother – the woman in the story – clear the stream, I used to think she was out of her mind. Who talks to and clears a stream?

Her conservation efforts were lost on me. The same way that every time she told me the best way to whiten teeth was to use charcoal, I thought she was being ridiculous. My educated mind could not relate to the wealth of traditional knowledge my grandmother had stored up. Knowledge built on real life experiences and passed down through traditional engagements.

Today, it is with great shame that I say that the stream no longer exists. My grandmother died in 2003. Today, the greatest craze in beauty and cosmetics is charcoal. Toothpaste, mask, conditioner you name it. It is all about charcoal. Why did I not appreciate my grandmother's knowledge and understanding of science? Is it just because she did not eloquently articulate her thoughts in English that I so comfortably speak? Is it because I allowed an alienation from what seemed like traditional knowledge to rob me of the opportunity to learn from someone who had tried and tested methods?

So, yes, our traditions matter!

Another great tradition that is relevant to development is marriage.

I have, on occasion, had the privilege of attending beautiful traditional marriage ceremonies. I am always taken by the extent to which the ceremony is really about bringing the two families together. I think it is a great tradition that binds our families, communities and society together. What I speak of is Ghanaian tradition. Such marriages are found in places across the continent but are not all the same.

The format of these marriages reinforces unity – exactly what we need if we are to make substantial progress.

Of course, for a new generation, there are modern twists to the ceremony. The formation dancing. The music that is local, yet so refreshingly present-day. The outfits that are a cross between traditional and modern. The decor that exudes finesse in a Ghanaian way.

I normally leave convinced that we have a lot that enriches our identity, sense of belonging and togetherness. We must celebrate these and protect them.

Sometimes, to change is to make what you have more relevant. Around the world today, we see the crossing over of traditions. Practices that used to belong uniquely to one region become globalised by being modernised, scaled up, communicated and sold on a large scale.

The fact that the same can be achieved with what is traditionally from Africa is not far-fetched.

Why is curry, a traditional dish from Asia, one of the most popular dishes in the UK? It was modernised to suit a different palate and scaled up by the many Asian restaurants who sell it. It is now heavily communicated and sold on a mass scale through large supermarkets.

Can we do the same? Of course. We already are. African print[5] has made it into the main stream by the designers who saw beyond the old styling approach (the traditional 'kaba and slit'[6]) to create modern styles. Our designers are still building scale. We can support them to go large.

The day I saw a trench coat made of African print in a luxury designer shop in Dubai I smiled – because 'we can' was becoming 'we are'!

For all this translation to become a reality, we must empower a generation.

I love to use my glass of water example.

Can I have a glass of water please? It is a question I have heard many times from my children. When they ask me to get them a drink, I willingly oblige; particularly if they are in the middle of a meal. All I ask is that they say *please* and show appreciation by saying *thank you.*

It is about our willingness to serve one another. I ask them to do things more frequently than they ask me. Yet I do not take for granted that they do the things I ask. Empowerment means showing our young generation that respect should be universal,

[5]What has typically been deemed as African print is largely non-African by source. However, the colourful patterns have become closely associated with African fashion.
[6]'Kaba & Slit' refers to a traditional ensemble for ladies

and they must also be willing to serve others accordingly. If they feel empowered because they are treated as such, they will be more likely to make meaningful contributions to the development of their countries. Meaningful contributions that will build their countries up to the legitimate members of an AU that truly represents the best of Africa. After all, wasn't that part of the premise of its formation?

I cannot move on from this topic without touching on the impact of independence celebrations. What is the meaning of this annual celebration to a young generation?

Take Ghana's national anthem as an example.

One of my favourite lines in the national anthem is "...and make our nation great and strong..."

As the song is sang, I reflect and ask myself, *how does a nation become great and strong*? How does it take its place in the *real* league of nations to be recognised as *Great and Strong*?

I believe that the only greatness a nation has is in the greatness of its people. The strength of a nation is in the strength of its people. I also believe that repeatedly playing out and rehashing independence persistently holds people hostage. Hostage to a repeated narrative of a conquered people finding their way. I feel it reinforces a notion of helplessness rather that the empowerment and strengthening it is supposed to promote.

Why do Canada, Australia, Singapore and the USA not have independence days but rather National Days? I suspect it has something to do with the psychology of what is celebrated.

History bears witness to the fact that it is great men and women who make nations *great and strong*. We must systematically encourage our young people to become great and strong in their own right. We must continue to allow each generation to stand on the shoulders of the previous generation to more greatness. To become greater and stronger than the generation that has been. We must create the right environment and change thinking to produce greatness and strength. We must lead by example.

Your personal greatness and strength are the best gifts you could offer your country!

With all this said, does having self-dignity matter for our greatness to lead to development?

Why do I ask? Well, because each day I see many acts that suggest to me that self-dignity is a challenge. That perhaps a lack of self-dignity undermines self-determination.

I once read an article about a group of young men who had crossed the Mediterranean from Africa to Italy. They were working as volunteers to clean the streets where they lived. Unemployed, they were willing to work for free in a foreign country.

I wondered how many would volunteer to clean their own countries in Africa!

Somehow, I doubted they would be willing to do so. For some reason, our own people continue to treat the one continent they were given as not worthy of their sacrifice. That their sweat is better used building and sustaining elsewhere. Why has this legacy of subservience persisted? Why do our people continue to feel inferior enough to treasure the other more than themselves?

Yet we live on a continent that is filled with people of faith. Faith that does not always include service and self-dignity. Every human being has faith in something and a choice of whom to serve and whether to have self-dignity.

By faith, I am specifically referring to belief systems. From a developmental point of view, I think we should make our faith more practical. Faith must be supported with action. In addition to believing, we must act in practical ways to make progress. Pray, plan and execute your plans to achieve your goals.

By service, I am referring to a willingness to do something for someone else; paid or unpaid. Our history has led us to a place where service is treated as menial. After generations of seeing service in the light of master and helper, service has become devalued in our eyes unless the right master is being served. We need to uplift the image of service by treating people who serve with respect. Life itself is about service. To develop collectively, we must learn to serve each other.

And we must have self-dignity. Many express this as an effect rather than a cause. I can see the value in that view. By holding demeaning views of people for being younger, less economically capable or less empowered, they learn to demean themselves. By abusing faith and making individual progress all about outcomes they don't control, they learn self-pity. All these lead to a lack of self-dignity.

So, let's have more practical faith, serve willingly like the master who washed feet, show appreciation and hold people up to dignified standards of what they are worth.

4

WE HAVE THE WOMEN

'African women are leaders.'

We must proudly celebrate African women. Our societies always had their own ways of celebrating women. Ways that have been eroded due to the over-characterisation of African women by the negative.

All too often, the African woman is viewed through the lens of struggle. Yet I am reminded of what we truly represent – proud industry. That so many African women confidently and proudly improve outcomes for those around them by working hard to make the most of themselves.

No longer must she be characterised by the loud volume of Female Genital Mutilation (FGM), child marriage and patriarchy, as many assume are the only experiences of African women. She must echo the hard work, nurturing and victories she has won.

And we have so many African women who are winners. These winners are crying out for, and pulling up, more winners.

Wangari Maathai, the late Kenyan Nobel Peace Laureate, once said "the higher you go the fewer women there are". This is true of both the developing and developed world. It tells a story of under-representation in decision-making and leadership roles across countries, not just in Africa.

The fact that a lack of women at the top robs us of the balanced view that gender diversity brings to leadership is a known fact that should be talked about in greater detail. Greater objective detail that focuses on creating positive outcomes and not for the sake of mere discussion. There is another side of this same coin, which is the fact that, even in leadership positions, many women are still treated as less-worthy peers. They are expected to be grateful for their inclusion, as though they did not work even harder than their male counterparts to get there. They are spoken to as subordinates by less qualified colleagues. Their ideas are discredited until those same ideas are articulated by a male colleague and then, suddenly, they are seen as the best ideas.

This is not an issue unique to Africa. Neither is it forcibly worse in Africa where matriarchal societies have existed for centuries.

The good news is that a lot of this stems from inherent biases in modern systems. It means it is possible to change attitudes as we deal with bias. It is possible for women to be respected as equal business leaders in their own right.

So, let us celebrate all women who persist in spite of the challenges. We should celebrate the men and women who make a conscious effort to put their biases aside and see abilities when dealing with a woman in all spheres of life. Making room for her makes room for the next woman. This is the time for men to boldly support women as they rise. Their achievements are the achievements of the entire society. Let us join hands to ensure that we get the benefit of our total capabilities and not just of one half of the population.

African women are leaders! I hope this statement stirs up greater conversation among people.

Africa's history is littered with stories of African women in leadership. We read about Ethiopia's Queen of Sheba and her ability to engage politically. We read of Ghana's Yaa Asantewaa and her battle cry. We read about Queen Nzinga of Angola, the colonial negotiator. These women led their people and today we still have African women in leadership positions.

Traditionally, domestic roles were clearly defined for good reason: to successfully nurture families and create prosperity through efficient use of resources. Roles were different but equally respected. Respect was at the heart of traditional roles – each leading family and society in ways that mattered. Among the Akan people of West Africa, male and female chiefs are dressed in gender neutral regalia. Their authority is not based on their gender.

I appreciate that there has been a degree of erosion in this description. In some cases, the structure has been completely abused and this no doubt has to be addressed. An evolved modern version that serves family, society and nation well in the African context is required.

But what about the workplace? The workplace is a by-product of education, since education is a pre-requisite for modern formal work. To fully address any form of discrimination in the workplace, we must fundamentally resolve discrimination in school. No longer should children be held back because of their gender, background, physical ability or any other form of diversity. School has to be a place where each child has the opportunity to maximise and realise their potential. A little girl should not be bullied for being smart! That, for instance, girls don't do science and math! Bias in formal education was imported to Africa as part of biases that had been built into schools in western countries, at inception.

Addressing the issues at school will ensure that the workplace is increasingly populated by leaders who have learnt to respect diversity. That people who feel different will be less likely to feel they cannot achieve their professional goals because school has taught them that they too can!

And, yes, I am particularly interested in what this means for young women. Young women, please think carefully about the socialisation that may have taught you that you are on the back foot at work, and challenge what you believe you are capable of. The world needs the absolute best you have to offer.

So how do we press for progress? What does progress mean to you?

For me, progress means that we have to build on what was and create improved outcomes for the next generation.

I have told many people the story of how none of my grandparents was educated. My father was the only one of his siblings to graduate from university, my mother the only one of her siblings to go to school. Yet, their achievements were a marked improvement on their parents' lives, thus laying a foundation that I could build on for my own life.

My grandmothers spent their lives raising families. My mother worked and raised her family. So, I have no excuse. None of us has an excuse. We must press for progress by taking action to realise our full potential.

I have many words for the woman that I am today – business leader, engineer, thought leader, wife and mum come to mind. There are many other facets to who I am all housed in the body of one woman.

No one should let their gender be a limitation. Live all the many facets that make you the amazing person you are.

There is power in "we can"!

Africa's sustainable development can only come from within. Which is why I have been committed to the fact that we must develop a psyche of 'we can'.

In 2016, six female business executives and CEOs – Freda Duplan, Pearl Esua-Mensah, Patience Akyianu, Edith Dankwa, Maidie Arkutu and Lucy Quist – decided that it was possible that we could form a network that would Inspire, Empower and Support female executives to grow their careers and make a difference both locally and internationally.

We decided it was possible for this organisation to matter not only to women but men who understand the benefits of self-actualisation. It is about self-actualisation for women and the positive impact this will have on our nation and continent.

The *Executive Women Network* was born. And, after months of hard work, we were able to reach out to other female executives to join us. We received support from many companies. After working behind the scenes for the best part of a year, on the 19th of April 2016 we were blessed with a full launch.

It took a lot of hard work, but it is a clear demonstration of the fact that it is possible to start from exactly where you are and create change through action. Today, years later, the organisation has grown and seen its members achieve many successes.

5

'...poverty...is the result of a system designed to produce poor people.'

WHAT IS THE CHANGE WE NEED?

The change we need is rooted in our actions of today.

Today is sometimes underrated, especially when it comes to our hopes and dreams. Perhaps, like me, you find it is easier to talk about what you will do in future and not what you are doing today. Maybe, calling our aspirations 'hopes and dreams' leaves us feeling that they belong to tomorrow. But today is all we have. Tomorrow, well who knows?

The most important time to create our success is today. Our choices, habits and attitudes of today will create tomorrow's success.

If you are thinking that the idea sounds basic, I agree with you; it is. However, the simplest things can be the most difficult to do. Consciously grabbing today sounds too simple but it can be a challenge.

One of the things I have come to find most baffling is how sometimes, despite great hopes and dreams, conversations persistently revolve around what is wrong in Africa. It is as though people will not bring themselves to genuinely believe in the possibility of real sustainable change. To bring themselves to believe today that a different outcome is possible. This comes across strongly in some of the social media conversations I find myself privy to.

Worst still, it is the informing undertone more often than not when I take questions at an event. It always starts along the lines that typically focus on "…the government of country Y spent X% of their budget on defence and not education. Why are African leaders so mean?" We quickly jump from the situation of one country to assume all countries are doing the same. Another example is "…the streets flood when it rains because the government is doing nothing about it".

Why is the solution always in someone else's hands? Why do people always remove themselves from the solution?

How about "I will engage policy makers, think tanks et al to discuss budgetary allocation and make it an important issue for the people in the next general election?" Or, "…the streets flood when it rains, today I am going to book a meeting with my local representative to see how we can reduce the impact of rain in my neighbourhood?" That is the essence of today! The ability to take control of the time and make it count for the future.

Being surrounded by poverty is not an accident. Neither is it a curse. Not at all. It is also not the result of limited human capacity as people keep suggesting. That same human capacity that was even less trained than today's generation did the work required to build many nations across the globe.

No, poverty is a systemic issue. It is the result of a system designed to produce poor people. Day one of life, we all take in a first deep breath. Even-keel. Every human being is on an even-keel. What happens next is all about your system. Who received you upon arrival into life? Who are your parents? They receive you with all their love. But what system do they live in? That is what will most likely determine your outcomes.

Just as poverty is the result of an input into a system to produce an output, prosperity is systemic. It is a system that starts in our minds. The minds of the families and communities we are born into.

Our minds are important. Our minds manage and pilot our system of success.

Our minds navigate external circumstances for our success. Our minds control our will to succeed. A success system requires consistency, focus and the absolute resolve to win. We can build personal, corporate and national systems of success. The real issue is *are we willing to choose to do so*?

We should consciously choose to live a success-creating system. To live it, we will have to be willing to create it. Not just learn from other systems around the world but craft systems relevant to our context that have a real chance of delivering success. We must also recognise and celebrate daily successes. Focus less on the not so successful events, just learn from them.

To be successful on a personal level, we have to define what that looks like. I have a busy schedule. But when I am able to spend time with people I care about, I feel I have succeeded. When I am able to consistently pray and meditate, I call that *success*. When I meet the day's business target, that is *success* for me. The small wins make me feel as successful as the big wins. The small wins create the big successes. So, in addition to having long term big goals for success as a business leader and family woman, I am acutely aware of the fact that my route to those successes depends on how I design and execute today.

It is relatively clear how this personal success translates into corporate success. As each professional succeeds in meeting their business targets, the company succeeds; as long as their performance indicators are aligned to the company's key performance indicators.

But how does this translate to national success? In my view, this is where the greatest paradigm shift is required. All too often, the context within which the transformation we want to see exists is forgotten. People forget the impact of the interruptions of history such as slavery, the struggles to adopt a system of governance such as democracy not based on our own history and the fact that changing so many people at the same time is a challenge. The assumption that national systems of success will come from elected leaders alone may single-handedly be the greatest tool of self-destruction.

So, first, we need to take in a deep breath. And as we breathe, we must think of the fact that the person we feel inside is a change leader. A change leader who wants to see their country do better and achieve more. What is that change leader's role?

Around the world, countries have succeeded when a generation believes that change is possible and lays a new foundation for future generations. Like Japan building national pride and growing into a global influencer at a time when many countries would have responded and accepted themselves as inferior.

Successes in recent times, even on a single issue, serve as a reminder to us that national success is possible.

I recall the story of Jamaican sprint success. Success that is built from the bottom up. Schools leagues. Races, in some cases, without training shoes. This approach became a sure way to identify the best athletes in the country. The process is repeated until the best bubble to the top and represent an entire small nation on a global stage. A global stage that values athleticism. Suddenly we look at the nation differently because we see positive representation of the best of its people. And, yes, there is an economic benefit. Its starts with the spillover of the work ethic it takes to succeed in athletics into personal and professional life. Then you have the revenue generation. Suddenly others want to learn from you. And, of course, there is prize money. Don't misunderstand me, athletic success did not suddenly develop the country but producing a global record holder tells the people that they too can.

Perhaps what we need to do is pick one challenge, make it national, get everyone to participate and demonstrate clearly what it takes to succeed in creating change.

For most countries of the continent, I can think of many unifying challenges to rally round. Pick your choice.

How about healthcare? Healthcare affects us all and requires a multidisciplinary approach which means we all can participate in improvements.

Healthcare is a fundamental need that affects the entire population. Perhaps it is our collective burning platform. An urgent need that has to be addressed because it affects us all. A need for all that undermines the very human capacity that we need to develop. The right infrastructure, professionals and understanding of primary healthcare all require our urgent attention. Mortality and disease statistics point to the fact that healthcare must drastically improve. Good healthcare must sustain us through a lifetime. We need greater productivity from each individual, so we need them to be healthy. Greater productivity that results in the economic growth we seek. We must see the issues for what they are and invest in a focused and sustained manner. Our commitment must be over a long period.

Our schools must teach in ways that we each at least understand our bodies better and take ownership of our own wellbeing through our daily choices. We must stop blaming preventable deaths on unseen hands - forces for which we have no redress. We must care for our local environment. Caring for ourselves and environment will lead us to care more about systemic processes. Processes that impact our wellbeing.

Focusing on and fixing one big national issue will empower us all to see change as possible. To accelerate, we all need to get on board. And we must take everyone along the journey with us. We need to live healthily for longer and be more productive if we are to create a prosperous continent!

That is just one example articulating a burning platform. There are many others. How about making good food affordably available to the entire population? Another burning platform.

In an environment that is starved of the type of infrastructure that allows decisions and actions taken at the highest national levels to impact people on a large scale, a few thousand elected officials cannot bring change to over a billion people. No, we need many more people who are willing to lead with a focus on creating a new Africa to succeed. Those leaders need a rallying call. A common focus of key priorities. As leaders, we must see ourselves in that picture. We must speak and think as creators of that picture. And if we think enough about it, we will act on it.

A key factor is *time*. Bluntly put, we need to change our relationship with time. We must place value on time. Real value.

Regardless of circumstance, there was a moment in the past when we each made our entrance into the world. And in that moment, we were vulnerable in every way except one – time

We each appeared with our full allocation of time. We don't know how long, but we got it. Time truly is all we have. The balance we strike in investing our time determines how well we maximise our outcomes in life, given our circumstances.

Our education is a conversion of our time into knowledge as we choose to invest our time in studying.

Our wealth is a conversion of our time into economic value as we choose to invest our time in profitable ventures such as work.

And, yes, some of the time we must invest in resting and relaxing; in building relationships by being together.

Time is everything. It is all we have. How much of our potential is realised is largely dependent on the choices we made with our time. So, our continent needs to place a premium on the truest of assets: the time each person has to make a meaningful contribution. Imagine what would happen if over a billion people suddenly chose to value time more. Not just *some* but the majority. What if we stopped joking about tardiness and decided that actually it was too high a price to pay on a development path that requires acceleration?

I try to have a consistent approach to each day – routine. And when the routine is disrupted, I live through the short-term disruption and focus on getting back on track. My routines have evolved over time, but I always have some form of routine. Without a routine I feel lost. My calendar is full of things I need to do on various dates to come. Just so I get things done.

We all need to create techniques that work for us to maximise what we get out of our time. It is an urgent call on a continent that can no longer afford to waste time.

Perhaps we need to compartmentalise our attitudes to time. Where can we be flexible and where not? I suggest that we should transition to using precise time in over 80% of our dealings. And, yes, it is the proverbial 80/20 thinking; but it is as good a start as any. The fact is, we need to do better at least 80% of the time for the results we need.

In addition to time, we need a refocus on *real results*.

When I first joined the telecommunications industry, I had the privilege of working for an extremely focused leader. He was appointed to transform the company across Africa.

It is amazing what we can learn from great leaders, if we are willing to do so.

One of his mantras to me was "It does not matter how well you dribble the ball. You have to score the goal to win". The truth is that, in a football match, we enjoy skillfulness of play, yet we quickly become impatient if our team consistently misses opportunities to deliver the real results – goals. At the end of the game, what we walk away with is the memory of goals won or lost because that is the real essence of the time spent.

I, in turn, have developed a habit of asking my teams: "Did you score the goal?"

I ask this, especially, when someone proceeds to give a long explanation about what they did and I cannot see a real result in sight. That is dribbling.

This was illustrated a few years ago quite clearly at the men's AFCON games. Remember the nail-biting final between Ghana and Cote d'Ivoire?

Ghana appeared to be the better side. They played really well. Most football pundits hold this view. Ghana played well. But! At the end of the day, the team that walked away with the trophy was the team that 'scored the goal', Cote d'Ivoire! Playing well is simply not enough.

We should never lose sight of performance. Success and progress have never come to me simply by how nice I sound. Or how well I played. They have always come by *delivering results*.

We have to hold ourselves to the delivery of goals. Only by holding ourselves to goals can we credibly set a tone of holding others to goals.

A focus on goals will help us change our engagement with elected officials.

As we work on our national goals, we must determine to meet acceptable global standards. The idea is not to meet the expectations of others, but really to meet our own expectations. In a connected world where access to information is as simple as breathing, our expectations of what is acceptable should meet the standards for any human being. I understand that not all information is accurate, but we must first seek out information to be in a position to make that judgement call. Our people have now rightly come to expect access to information. They use this information to make choices about how they access opportunities. Why else would people be willing to risk their lives to cross the Mediterranean? It is for two reasons: their mindset that their countries cannot be fixed and their belief that people elsewhere unanimously live a better standard.

When I worked as the CEO of Airtel in Ghana, we organised *Speaker Series* led by successful women for International Women's Day. Well, we made it a whole month, but I digress. These amazing ladies shared their stories with both male and female staff to inspire us to greatness.

One of the speakers shared that a key to her success is working to global standards and not settling to operate at a level that is only relevant locally. She said that is how she stood out every time. I fully agree with her.

We need to seek out what is required globally and work to that standard to stand out. We create globally-appreciated value this way.

I recall a week in which history was made. It got my applause and quite frankly I still applaud this man.

Trevor Noah, a South African comedian from Soweto, was named as the successor to Jon Stewart, the American comedian who hosted *The Daily Show* in the USA! His diaspora move was out of Africa to tackle serious issues; with a lot of humour, of course.

At the time of his move, I had only seen Trevor on *The Daily Show* when he went to talk about Ebola during the crisis of 2014/2015. I do not know whether it was his first visit, but I was impressed by what I saw.

This is not someone who can be dismissed as an outlier. Yes, he has become one; but he did not start out as one. What really matters is that something about how he operates has earned him a job many miles away from where he grew up. And I continue to follow his show. I recently watched an interview of him with the rest of the team talking about their creative process, particularly given the erratic nature of the USA's political discourse under the leadership of its 45th president. I was impressed. The work ethic that creates sustainable success is the same wherever you find yourself. Those rules of real engagement are the same.

It is my vision of a new Africa that these changes will lead to real transformation.

> *"Transformation is up to each and every one of you. There are no shortcuts."*

I borrow these words from a truly transformational leader to remind us of our collective responsibility. They are words from a message in which President Paul Kagame talked about how we deserve better than living off the wealth of others. He talked of how we have all we need to transform our nations.

Living off the wealth of others is not just about international wealth but, more importantly, locally doing our part and not waiting for the wealthy we encounter in society to provide for us. When we each transform our lives, our nations, by extension, will also be transformed.

Without belabouring the point, the traumatic events of Rwanda in 1994 are well-documented. I first visited the country in 2009 and have visited often ever since. What I experience consistently is a nation of people who are willing to create a *bold new* country for themselves. They believe they truly have all it takes to succeed, what they need to do is work together towards that outcome. It is the focus and the staying power of the people, young and old, that I admire the most. When a nation of people is determined, real change happens.

Real change happened because their labour is geared towards productive change.

That productive labour releases the power of real human potential.

What value do we place on the power of the potential of the people who labour?

A few years ago, I had the honour of watching Dr. Patrick Awuah speak. He is the founder and President of Ashesi University. I have subsequently had the pleasure of engaging him more personally. He said something so profound that day that rang in my ears and has stayed with me. He said that when he was leaving Microsoft, it had about 30,000 employees who generated more wealth for the company than the GDP of Ghana! Ghana, with over 20 million people at the time, had an output lower than a company of 30,000 people! I still find the comparison astounding. It is the sort of mathematics that leaves a problem in my mind to solve. To put it another way, more recently Apple was valued at over $1trillion at one point in 2018. This makes Apple worth *over* 1% of global GDP which is in stark comparison to Sub-Saharan Africa's 3% of global GDP!

Hearing these facts also reminds me so much of why I believe only we can realise our potential. Why the change we need can only come if we each realise our potential.

Not mineral resources. Not the natural advantage of the weather. Those are assets we can use, part of the means but not the determinants.

Harnessing our creative mental abilities, working hard through our labour and focusing on our visions...that is what will change our nations.

So, as we join hands to build the new future, let's celebrate the immense power of our potential and be filled with excitement that we are going to achieve the vision together.

Along the way we must celebrate progress.

Progress means we are moving closer to our vision. It means getting one more thing right. Another milestone achieved.

I believe that, as we focus on our ultimate goals, we have to also acknowledge the steps in between. Celebrating progress means that our effort and energy commitments feel well-spent.

Celebrating progress also means that we recognise how far we have come. When you think of many African countries, we must be able to apply perspective. Perspective that makes us appreciate how far we have come. Perspective that energises us to work harder together; for therein lies our greatness.

So, whatever the noise around us is, we must remember that we are making progress and that may be what counts the most on days when we feel the task is too great.

It is how we build the strength to deal with curveballs.

I once had a comment on my social media pages. It was a response to a question I asked about what needs to be done. The response read "Africa has a long way to go!"

Despite the seeming realism of this statement, what bothers me most is the pessimism I sensed in it. I assume the person meant *in comparison to the rest of the world.* If so, I wondered, how do you measure *long*? I ask this question because if we are to realise our potential together, we must align on our common big goal. For a young person who needs things to work right now, the mindset of *long way* can be treacherous.

Africa has many things going well. When I travel the world, I see firsthand that every country has its own challenges. Large swathes of population left behind on various human indicators. Yet, if we view the countries outside Africa only through the filter of what is presented to us, we develop an unrealistic sense of what they have and how they live. As this book is not an attempt to normalise what is, I will refrain from naming specifics. A simple internet search will demonstrate how poverty, both economic and emotional, and other ills such as child marriage, have seemingly been allowed to become part of brand Africa. And, yet, they exist in the most developed of nations. We need to better showcase and communicate what African people have.

The continent's journey is tied to the journey of its people. That is why we should focus on helping our people go on the *long way* journey.

And if we have a long way to go, then we need speed. We need to value our time and fill life with progress. Create a sense of urgency. We need to apply a sense of urgency to our forward movement.

We too can and must build solutions that work well for us. Only we know how.

A few years ago, I had the privilege of going on my first ever trip to Morocco. A beautiful country with a lot of built infrastructure right here on our lovely continent of Africa. But that is not what struck me the most. It was the market place that got me. You see in this hot country the market places were constructed in a simple way that ensured that the afternoon heat was kept at bay while allowing sufficient light to filter through. I visited two markets and they were the same.

It was clearly a solution to their very own local conditions!

We need to increasingly create solutions that respond to our own needs, not just copy-paste approaches. The truth is that *copying and pasting* has been the bane of the continent's progress. All too often when copied solutions don't work, people are left baffled. In such cases we seem to forget that contextual adaptation, led by the people who live the Africa experience, may be what is needed. Or more importantly, that we must create specific solutions - harder work but perhaps more sustainable. The human path to economic evolution is not a one size fits all path. The global narrative leaves most people thinking that developed African countries will forcibly look like developed western countries. How could that even be possible when the environment, histories and human experiences are different? Why the over-simplification?

Perhaps the greatest pillar in changing our approach to create real change is education. If we are to create a system that delivers true success, our academic and social curricular must become more geared towards moulding minds ready for the change they may execute. Some wholeheartedly criticise education in many African countries. I do not fully agree. First, because the broad-brush approach does not work for me but also because I, like many of my peers, studied in the same system. In many cases, there is content that is pedagogically relevant. The real issue to me is the contextual relevance.

Minds that continually learn, evolve, challenge the status quo and produce sustainable solutions – these are what we must produce. That is the kind of education we need.

My father, who is in his 70s now, received that same education to become an engineer and worked in many countries. However, he was educated at a time when there was less strain on the education system because there were fewer children. Many of his generation achieved better academic outcomes which allowed them to become architects of creating their country's future. It also was the case that the world of business was different in their time. There was less complexity. So, the need for changes to contextualise education is not only an African challenge. The challenge to provide more material to support education may arguably be more acute in many African countries. It is why I believe that clearly defining the issues and articulating what the real root causes are is important. We must refrain from looking at challenges as though there are no challenges in other places, define in detail and resolve.

Order, organisation, planning, diligence, adherence to rules, excellence and integrity are needed as we continue on this journey of creation.

And then there are curveballs! Going back to the Accra gas explosion of June 2015, that was a huge curveball. On that day, according to some media outlets, half the expected rain for the month in some parts of the country came down in just a few short hours.

Accra, the coastal lying capital city, bore the brunt of this – the reported devastation captured it all. Flooding, gas station explosion and the attendant loss of life were too much to bear. It was an unexpected curveball insofar as the rainfall was concerned. It was a manmade curveball as far as drainage and response to flooding were concerned. It is a clear example of a dramatic challenge along the journey. It is one that people will remember for a long time.

Remembrance must serve a purpose that travels forward in time. Yes, remembrance gives us the chance to express our regret at the loss of life, but the lessons must not be forgotten.

If drains were clear, illegal structures were disallowed and health and safety mattered more, perhaps we will be remembering a different story.

I share this example of a curveball because, in the journey of creating *the bold new normal* for Africa, there will be unexpected dramatic challenges along the way. These are points of inflexion – when collective emotion can be harnessed to implement dramatic change.

This flood experience could have led to a detailed report with recommendations. The recommendations could have squarely focused on planning enforcement, more stringent adherence to environmental regulations and clearer education on flood response. However, the most visible change was a short-term response to health and safety regulatory adherence by fuel stations that was short-lived. We have to see things through.

6

'To create wealth for Africa, we must ensure that African money spends most of its time in Africa.'

A Generation Leading The Way

This current generation is a generation of Africans who have been sold the promise of democracy. Ghana, among other countries, has been applauded as a beacon of democracy and so perhaps a good proxy for that path. Yet, Ghana's journey of maturity is playing out differently for different generations. Particularly, my mind was drawn to how evolving governance impacts the generation that experiences it for the first time. It is after all, part of the evolution of what should be in the new Africa.

Three distinct groups came to mind.

My parents' generation were the school children who saw Ghana gain independence from colonial governance. My mother was in Class 3 at the time and tells us stories of being a proud *young pioneer*, as they were called. How similar was it for the young Nigerian, Kenyan or Congolese at the time? Even though the movement was driven by dissatisfaction and a desire for self-actualisation, I wonder how many of the structural issues of the past era were addressed.

My generation saw Ghana move into democracy. It was while I was in secondary school that the talk of the change intensified, took shape and happened. I, like many young people at the time, was not sure what that change would bring but, somehow, we trusted that it was a good thing. It had to be! Suddenly, it meant that young people had a voice that would not be ignored. But have they been heard?

Today, there is a generation after us. They are a generation that has only known many countries in Africa as democratic. For them, *free and fair* is to be expected. It is how things are done! But how have their lives been impacted?

Ghana may have led the way but the continent as a whole has come a long way on the governance path since those heady days of struggling for self-determination. I know this because I have read of similar changes around the world. What took hundreds of years in self-governing countries around the world took a matter of decades in Africa. We must recognise this progress particularly as the change in governance was essentially another importation that continues to jar against historical norms of governance on the continent.

That first generation, my parents' generation, took a leap of faith into self-rule. There was no blueprint on the continent because, as Ghanaians, they were the first. They would have to learn from countries outside Africa, largely out of context, but also endure the unique challenges that were to come given our history. Given the huge expectations created.

My generation was led into democracy. Into an era where we could speak up and have our say. Again, a new frontier which came with ups and downs but worth the journey. What were the messages passed down? Whose shoulders were we to stand on? What was the vision? My parents' generation were clear and aligned on the vision – that is why they were young pioneers. Subsequent orchestrated disruptions in the form of coup d'états created a sense of self-preservation that took eyes off the greater goal of creating the future for their grandchildren. The message was not passed on. The message changed to looking after one's own. That is what my generation heard going into democracy.

But this current 21st century young generation! This young generation lives the normalcy of democracy. This generation is special. Their African-ness means they remain pioneers on the continent. Just like their grandparents before them. This generation lives in democracies that are maturing. This generation must be the generation that lifts Africa up to global standards. This must be the beacon generation that takes Africa on that journey.

Our future, our continent, is this generation. So, let's keep doing all we can to strengthen the foundations on which they build. Let's lead them to realise their potential and become the greatest leaders of the most richly-endowed continent on this planet.

The new African of this generation must become a truly global citizen and cease to be a pariah to be turned away.

A Bell Rings for Africa

The perspective of young professionals in Africa must be global. The boundaries of Africa should not limit where our young people believe they can go with their ideas just like young people around the world see Africa as accessible for them to explore their ideas.

Not so long ago, I encountered and read about the ***She Leads Africa*** team with great pride. This team of bright young people rang the closing bell of the New York Stock Exchange!

This was a source of great pride for me on three significant levels.

First, this team is led by two very bright young women, Yasmin Belo-Osagie and Afua Osei, who are empowering female business leaders across the continent. By extension, they are setting an example for all business leaders. They demonstrate that the world is truly their oyster.

Secondly, it is a pan-African organisation founded by a Nigerian and a Ghanaian. Yes, indeed, we can work together on large-scale initiatives across the continent. They show that real pan-Africanism that creates economic benefits is possible. It is how we will harness the strength of a large population.

Finally, they changed the game! Many years ago, I was part of the leadership team of a company that had interests across the continent. The opportunity arose for the company to ring the closing bell at the NYSE. Much to my dismay, not a single African from the leadership team was included in the team that flew to New York. The significance of this was not lost on me. Particularly because there was more than one African who could have gone, and the interest being represented was their business in Africa. African money without African people! Sadly, we are still faced with representations of African money without African people.

Today, we have new inspiration. We must continue to create businesses. We must address unmet needs. We must continue to work hard to realise our potential. We must take opportunities to demonstrate our contribution to the world because the new African is a global game-changer.

We must start to place the right value on what Africa produces. For this reason, we must choose carefully how we spend our money. Do you ever wonder where your money goes? How long does $1 spent in Africa stay in Africa?

Money is a store of value. I remember that definition from school. It represents value creation. So, what really happens when we spend our money? Well, a lot of it is spent at the retail level. If the goods and services we buy are made in Africa, then the retailer uses that money to pay the African wholesaler. If the inputs the wholesalers use are from Africa, then in turn the money goes to the input providers.

For example, if we buy soap made in Africa, the retailer will pay the soap producer who in turn will pay the people who provide the raw material which will most likely end up with a farmer (as most African soap is made from natural plant extracts). Notice that I made no mention of who owns the steps in the value chain, just where they get their inputs from. So, the soap can be made on a large scale in a big factory. If that plant is local, that is good for Africa as the workers, raw material providers, et al., get a part of that money. Of course, there are margins along the value chain but that is still value that can stay as this becomes someone else's income to spend.

Conversely, if that good or service is not from Africa, after the retailer the value of our money leaves Africa. I am sure you get the picture from my soap analogy. Yes, we must own businesses, but we must also own the responsibility of wise choices. Choices that grow our economies.

To create wealth for Africa, we must ensure that African money spends most of its time in Africa. That it changes hands here and circulates to support value creation. As we use our spending power to encourage African producers to create value, a lot of things change. We create incentives for them to improve quality. We give them reason to employ more people. We help them to create the bases for future innovations.

In a global world, we will always have goods and services from around the world. Yet, when faced with the choice, supporting the African producer matters. It is using our purchasing power to influence economic activity. It is a conscious bold new way to move Africa to sustainable growth. Let us change the script.

How about the Young African?

It is impossible to have a focused discussion about the new African without talking about our millennial generation. At a conference a while ago, a millennial defined being a millennial as 'a mindset'! She went on to explain that it is a mindset on how they engage with the world. I can see the truth in that. Millennials are perhaps the most talked about and documented generation to have ever lived.

But who is the African millennial? What will be some of the key factors that determine sustainable career success for their generation and beyond?

I looked up who the world calls a *millennial.* The term generally refers to someone born in the 1980s up to the early 2000s. That generation is supposedly characterised by a more liberal upbringing compared to their parents' generation. Millennials experience a heavy interaction with technology and have high expectations of what they will achieve in life.

I wondered how much of this definition applied to this generation in Africa. Did so many African parents become more liberal or did they largely sustain the upbringing they were used to? Are they all interacting with technology or are they more conscious of the cost of funding that interaction? Does the African millennial expect to change the world or hope that they will at least change their own outcomes?

I came to the conclusion that loosely calling this younger generation in Africa millennials is ok as long as we recognise their unique African experience. That, for them, cultural norms of their position in society are still relevant. They are curious about technology, but do not all have unlimited access to the use of technology. And, yes, some of them want to change the world yet others are still looking to leadership to create structures and pathways for them. Some are still young while many are now adults and parents in their own right.

I believe that we have a generation of young potential to harness in creating *The Bold New Normal* of a prosperous Africa.

Harnessing their potential requires that they are self-aware and develop themselves. That they understand self and place in their community to influence positive change.

It brings to mind my experience when I had the unique privilege of spending an afternoon with a YALI[7] Regional Leadership Centre West Africa cohort. It was a room full of determined young leaders from across the continent. I loved the sight of young leaders determined to make bold decisions and create a bold new continent together. We discussed some real challenges to achieving that.

Some of the questions we explored were:

- Is it easier or harder to lead in Africa and why?
- How does a leader manage activity versus productivity to make the continent more productive?
- How do you as a leader deal with the inconvenience of long-winded processes? Do you stay ethical, experience them and work to change them or do you cut corners and never make plans to fix the process?

I share this experience because I believe these are relevant conversations happening across many meetings on the continent. Yet, many people continue to feel alone in their efforts. Perhaps we need to use the many social engagement opportunities to rather focus on joined up conversations. Big conversations.

One such conversation is what I call 'the fallacy of independence celebrations'. My thoughts stem from the lack of clarity I have

[7] Young Africans in Leadership Initiative

when it comes to the purpose of the celebration. That lack of purpose means that, in addition to a reminder of the generation that moved for independence, the celebrations reinforce and pass on the narrative of a people who did not rule themselves. It is a narrative that cuts short our history and weakens resolve in the face of a complex world.

My history is older than any country in a post-colonial Africa. My history is of empowered proud Asante and Ga people. It is a history that includes an old empire of Ghana and even further back. It is a complex history.

I love to hear stories of my lineage. I hold on to them and cherish them. Typically, the story of my mother's lineage is told around her grandfather who was the chief of the village where she was born. A hardworking, wealthy leader who was committed to the well-being of the people in his village. I never had the privilege of meeting him, but I am told he had a particular message he repeated to his grandchildren. They were each to live in ways that ensured that they were never called before a jury and never work as bonded servants.

Servitude is where it gets interesting. His mother was a servant. I doubt she was bonded as her sons went on to achieve many things. Maybe she didn't earn much or had other issues associated with the absence of full freedoms. At least her children were free. However, she was not a southerner, maybe not even from modern day Ghana. We all know she was from up north - northern Ghana or Burkina Faso. We wish we knew more about her. We settle for telling each other that we have one more language to learn, we just have to figure out which one.

Ultimately, knowing this about just one ancestor reminds me of the fact that we are more joined up in the fluidity of our origins than we realise.

Independence, just like colonisation, was a point of inflection. A sharp change that can disorient for generations. I want my children to know this. Their lineage and history are more than just a few decades old. They go back millennia.

60 odd years makes it sound ok not to believe in self. After all, "we are a young nation", some may say. "Give us time. We will get there".

Acknowledging a longer dated history gives us all reason to believe in ourselves. And, in particular, I celebrate Ghana. She is the leader. The beacon nation of a continent, inspiring me to pay homage by leading too.

That leadership means responsibility. A responsibility to show the way. To show that her age will not deter her people from working together to move forward. To give up complaints and roll up sleeves to work diligently. Diligent work to weave together a masterpiece of a nation.

This short ode to Ghana is one I hope every reader will write for their own country. You can take a moment to do so right now. Each country needs its people to believe that they are enough.

And how is this relevant to my YALI conversation? Well, leadership in any country comes with its own contextual nuances. The same way that some leaders find ways to rally a nation behind a vision in other parts of the world can be applied to leading a country in Africa.

If we make productivity the goal in our discourse, we will focus our minds on activities that deliver the vision.

And processes? Well, as a new entrepreneur, I am experiencing the inconvenience of long-winded processes. I count myself fortunate as an experienced professional that I can engage to improve. Taking that responsibility should help pave the way for younger entrepreneurs who may not have the opportunity to influence the process to benefit from improvements.

Together, they all form a generation leading the way.

A young generation of hope.

7

'What exactly are we hungry for?'

THE CHANGE WE NEED

How are we going to change and create the Africa we all believe is possible? Think about all the things we wish were better – affordable food for all, an end to corruption, better sanitation, prosperity!

Sometimes, as I reflect on change, my thoughts turn to me. I wonder how much I am doing and what more I can do to contribute to the creation of that Africa; because we are not where we used to be, but not yet where we should be.

You see, we can only create change if we are willing to start with ourselves. Great change is never comfortable. It is only realised by confident leading. Being critical of others is all too easy – a superficial deflection. What if we decided to address root cause issues? What would we do if we discovered that, at the level of root causes, we are part of the problem?

Will integrity win the day by you saying *no* to the gift from the uncle you know cannot afford to give without being corrupt elsewhere or will you turn a blind eye to his source?

Will responsibility win by cleaning up our own neighbourhood to create the sanitation we want to see, or will we sit back and blame the authorities?

Will prosperity be born out of hard work that is consistent and thus sustainable, rather than quick gain that does not transcend generations because it is easily squandered?

None of these are easy tasks, yet our continent must realise its potential. It will only happen if we are willing to be the change we want to see!

Democracy affords us the right of an equal say in who is in charge. But is that the entirety of the significance of a vote? Every vote is a pledge. A pledge to work every day, regardless of who wins the election, to build your country. We each have a role to play in that building process.

In my early years of secondary school, I spent a lot of holidays in my mother's village under the care of my aunt and my grandmother who have both sadly passed away. My grandmother was meticulously hardworking. She had no formal education, but her routines were set. The sun never rose before her compound was clean. Her father had been the first settler in the village and, thus, the village chief. I mention him in an earlier chapter.

My grandmother was a conservationist. She was progressive. Ensuring that her surroundings, village and family made progress was a no-brainer to her. The grandchildren who attended day school always woke up to a pot of hot water boiling to ensure that they comfortably washed before school. The simple things like planning our meals in advance were covered. Saving so that she could afford to chip in for her grandchild was second nature. How did she make money when she could not physically manage a farm? She would gather firewood and take it to the market to sell. In the heat of the afternoons, when it was too hot for more strenuous tasks, she would sit behind her giant stone tablet and crack the shells of palm kernels to release the valuable nut. I would watch as she meticulously did this, one nut at a time, and fill a large container. She always had money to buy what she needed and some more for her grandchildren who all had parents of their own.

Of Faith and Mindset

I recount these simple acts because they represent a mindset. A mindset of independence. A mindset that says I will make the most of whatever is in my hand. Whatever skill I have, I will make use of it right here and now.

Government will always be an important lead in our development but what we think, say and do will and will count for more. We are the system that drives the country!

So, let our votes be our pledges to build on what we have. To build Africa – one country at a time.

As we vote, we should ask ourselves "what exactly are we you hungry for?" Our hunger influences our choices. Our hunger is determined by what we choose to prioritise. *We prioritise what we value most.* In that moment of voting, what is our greatest priority?

Has a curtailed history created a curtailed view of our future? What happened to our ancestors who thought trans-generationally?

Admittedly, daily life is not easy for many; but have you heard the story of the person who thought they had nothing because they had one outfit until they met the person who was naked? If you are reading this, then you certainly are not one who has nothing. For one thing you have access to information.

Short term thinking driven by immediate need, whether personal or in business, will not get us far. Indeed, Africa needs young business people who will think long term and take bold giant steps to create prosperous outcomes for the continent. A prosperous continent can only be built on prosperous individuals and prosperous businesses.

In Ghana, people sometimes like to say they are getting by 'small small'. We must change this language and change our mindset to make bold strides to achieve our visions. Let's get along 'big big'.

After all, most Africans profess a commitment to faith. Why have small aspirations when you have big faith? It is impossible to talk about development in Africa and not touch on faith.

But what is the role of faith in development? What role does faith play in our progress? What is the practical impact of faith on you? I ask because national development is usually an output of individual progress.

I have a number of questions on my mind for which I would appreciate your input. Perhaps you will write to me about your views.

I am a woman of Christian faith.

As I made my way home from church one day, I wondered to myself: *if we have held faith for generations, prayed for generations and believed for generations why are we where we are?* Why do I look out and see development gaps in all aspects of life?

Let me explain a little further.

When I see refuse on streets I ask myself: *what happened to cleanliness being close to godliness?*

When I see people waiting for someone else to fix their issues I ask: *what happened to the potential God has given them?*

When I hear stories of how an old person who is ill gets limited attention in hospital because 'they have had their time', I wonder whether I have a different reference point on the sanctity of human life.

So, without pointing fingers at others, what is the role of faith in your contribution to building your country and continent?

Our faith must be practical. Our actions must reflect our beliefs. We are empowered to dominate the earth as human beings so why allow circumstances to get the better of us?

One day on my way to church, I was stopped by a woman carrying an infant. I had just parked in the car park walking to the main entrance. The woman carrying the infant was a beggar and she asked me for money. My immediate reaction was to think *I don't have any change* and kept walking. Then I asked myself: *Why does the woman begging only deserve my change*? Surely, giving this woman a bank note was not a fortune so why not a bank note? If I will freely give in church, why can't I give to her?

I stopped and handed the woman a high bank note. The woman begging was shocked. Her eyes opened wide and she could not thank me enough. We were both clearly surprised at what had just happened and parted ways.

I thought deeply about what had just happened and realised that, all too often, Africa is treated as the beggar in my real-life story. We assume that current circumstances mean that a little more is enough. That just by improving things a little, many Africans should be content. Even many Africans themselves don't feel deserving of a life where they truly have the chance to prosper.

Why is this the case? Why is a little more enough for Africa?

Why do we want to eradicate poverty instead of create prosperity? Prosperity is where people can take life into their own hands and thrive because the basic building blocks are in place.

Faith may be common to large groups but one of the greatest assets the continent has is its diversity. Diversity that goes beyond the physical and really appreciates individuality.

Our individual identities greatly influence how we do what we do. The outcomes we create are products of our learned abilities and all the experiences that make us who we are.

The Power of the Individual

The unique identity that each person brings allows for the creation of an enriched team that is able to look at situations from a broad perspective and seek the best possible solutions. It is good for progress in any sphere and great leaders should always seek to build diverse teams.

Unfortunately, sometimes diversity is used as a reason to exclude rather than include people for better outcomes.

Gender diversity is most spoken about because it is a simple binary measure that is determined at first glance. But when we see people through the lens of their gender, what else are we missing about them? Isn't gender just the tip of the iceberg of who they are above the waterline? What calls are we making on what they are capable of?

When you think of yourself, do you only see yourself as being defined by who you are told you are? Don't allow yourself to be measured purely by a singular identity of any form. There is more to you than that single characteristic. How will you let your gender complement all your other strengths to demonstrate the unique you?

Don't let one aspect of your identity define you. Society needs *all of you* to contribute to the creation of bold new outcomes.

The subject of diversity is important when it comes to truly creating prosperous outcomes. Different skills and experiences come to bear. Different perspectives matter.

Most of all, it matters because each unique person contributes to the creation of unique and specific solutions.

When you have a problem, what do you do? The best person to solve a problem is the person who experiences it. This has been the case for problem solving and opportunity creation across the globe. So, why is an assumption made that solutions will come by others coming to save the African continent?

To create *The Bold New Normal* for a prosperous Africa, it is important that we embrace the circumstances that have uniquely brought us to this point – the same way you would for yourself as an individual. Understanding helps us formulate solutions that are appropriate.

Copied solutions don't last because they don't address the root causes of issues. Sustainable positive development comes from addressing the heart of issues.

So, don't let opinions make you feel less than. Embrace all that is you, so you can fully participate in creating the solutions the continent needs to prosper!

I once had the chance to write about how uniquely we are placed to solve our own problems and challenged people to think and behave like they have no limits. No more was I reminded of this than when I spoke to Form 3 students at a school in London. I passionately believe that young people all over the world have what it takes to reshape our world for the better. They have to believe that they are uniquely placed to do so and that it is possible.

So, again, I ask: what would you do if you had no limits? What is your vision of the future of Africa? What are you willing to uniquely create?

Outcomes in education!

Early one morning, before 6 am, I was out and about when I saw two sisters making their way to school. They were already on their way so early. The older one must have been in junior high school, the younger one class 2 at most. As I observed them, I thought of the millions of African school children doing the same. I thought of those who have done so for decades. In my heart, I was so proud of their determination and effort. I was inspired by the thought that they get up early each day to make one more day of self-improvement.

Then I recalled a conversation I had on an occasion before this day. The conversation was about the appropriateness of the instruction children were getting at school; in some cases, out of date and out of touch with what they need to prosper as adults. Useful for instruction but not entirely future-focused just as I mentioned a few pages ago.

Question the Knowledge

Isn't it sad, in fact unfair, that our children make such a great effort yet many of the adults involved in educating them don't care enough to reward their effort with good instruction? Why should they make all this effort every day and not be rewarded with top quality education?

On another occasion I heard a radio presenter say education is all the same. That it does not matter where people get their qualifications, wherever is the same. If we are going to solve real problems, we cannot wish them away in ignorance.

That day, the radio presenter really upset me. We must stop misinforming people in our ignorance. It is not all the same. And we should know that, judging by the outcomes we see around us. It is a challenge of quality and productivity. These children put in so much effort and it is time to fully reward them for it.

We need a *Bold New Normal* in education. We need education that inspires the mind to greatness. We need education that is relevant to the needs of each country and continent in the 21st century. Sound pedagogy is no longer enough. We need education that provides appropriate skills to young people who sweat to get through a tough system.

No more time for excuses. No more applause for mediocrity and the expectation of being given an easy pass to recognition because of *our situation.* Let's rather demand more. Human potential is evenly distributed around the globe. The outcome is determined by what you choose to do with that potential.

A question for you…if you had the power to reform education, what would you do and are you willing to be part of the change? Would you be a passive parent or one who actively engages in their children's school to improve education? Would you make your voice count?

Made in Africa

What is any African country's largest product contribution to the world? Let's think...Cocoa? Gold? Iron ore? Oil? What is your pick?

My answer? None of the above.

Africa's greatest contribution to the world is her people. When you think made in Africa, how often do the people come to mind?

I once asked a room full of university students whether they would pay more for a chemically-laden imported moisturiser or a locally-processed natural moisturiser. They generally chose the chemically-laden product. I asked why and they said chances are that a lot of research and skill had gone into the chemically-laden moisturiser.

Imagine that! They were willing to trust the chemically-laden moisturiser because they believed in the capacity of the people who made it. Then I asked them which they thought was better for them. They all said chances were that the more natural local product was better. How did we get to the point of rejecting what is local even when it is clearly better?

What Africa truly produces is her people. The first and largest product is the African person! It is time to place value on that person.

So, how do we create a prosperous Africa? By maximising the value we extract from her greatest resource – the people.

The responsibility lies with each of us to make the most of ourselves and support those around us to make the most of themselves to all realise our potential.

We must stop treating our people and their creations as less than.

To create these building blocks, we need better productivity!

Once, when I watched a programme about random infectious diseases, I was struck by the words of one victim. She said her ailment started with sleepiness. This led her to fall asleep at her desk at work. She said not doing her fair share of work made her feel guilty!

It got me wondering. How many people feel bad when they are not performing at work? Does your conscience speak to you when you don't get the work done on time? Do you feel guilty when you waste precious work time? On a continent where we have so much to solve, build and establish, we should hold each other to greater productivity.

Over the years, I have been part of many discussions on productivity. The level of output in Ghana, and Africa for that matter, should be much higher than it is. Yet it remains relatively low.

I am not saying people are lazy or inactive for that matter. People can be actively busy yet not productive if not focused on the delivery of a goal. And then there are the real time-wasters. Every time we walk into an office and people are watching TV, that is a scene of lowered productivity. Other culprits are the numerous unsolicited messages that create distractions and steal productive time from the recipients.

My musings led me to school children yet again. Even their productivity is reduced when their day is not structured around getting the most out of their education. They end up needing more time for their work and panic when they have to take exams because their time has not been spent well enough.

The fact is we need to produce greater output if we are to accelerate development. And, to do so, everyone has to learn to make the most of their time. Value time and use it wisely. Plan what you want to achieve and focus on achieving it. Politely turn down distractions!

The bold new Africa needs to regain some of our ancestral work ethic. The work ethic that made them labour even for others.

8

'As leaders, we must set the bar much higher for this continent.'

A New Vision

It is time to recognise a new vision of yourself. It is a privilege to be you. You are not just one of many. It is a privilege to be you because there is only one of you.

The circumstances of your birth were not within your control but what you choose to do with your life is absolutely within your control.

So instead of thinking of yourself as being born poor, think of yourself as being born with a whole lot of potential that you have to realise! Your potential is your prosperity.

Why does this matter? Because you are uniquely designed to fulfil a role that no one else can. So, if for any reason you have been left feeling insignificant, I encourage you to boldly re-imagine you. Take your strengths and ask yourself: *what am I going to do with them*? How am I ensuring that I personally embody *The Bold New Normal?*

We will only make sustainable progress in building a prosperous continent if we all get involved, and that includes you!

Transformation: we need big dreams to transform Africa for good.

I had the privilege of delivering the commencement speech for Ashesi University College's class of 2016 graduation. It is an institution from which I continue to draw inspiration. I left confident that if such bright people are part of us, we will transform Africa! I look forward to the day when Ashesi will be part of our new norm and not an outlier. To rise or to prosper? Africa needs to decide which it will be. It is this new generation's call to determine which it will be.

To rise is to improve, no matter how small the improvement. An improvement is an improvement. But to prosper? That requires definition, ambition, courage and drive. That requires real action that may be uncomfortable and challenging.

We continue to talk about leadership across the continent. But the question of whether we rise or prosper may be the ultimate leadership question for leaders in Africa in all aspects of society.

A couple of years ago at church, as I listened to the sermon, the question of Africa's small GDP was highlighted – and the penny fully dropped.

I did some research. IMF's data shows that Africa's contribution to global GDP in 2013 was 3.5%.

3.5%!

3.5% of global GDP means so many things. We all know, and many of us can see, what it means to people who live in Africa. But here are a couple of things that have occurred to me.

- It means an economic value below many single countries. Imagine, an entire continent's contribution being valued below a single country's.
- This implies that, for many global businesses, Africa's contribution may not actually count as much as the contribution of a country.

3.5% does not matter enough. Not when we are talking about over a billion people!

As leaders, we must set the bar much higher for this continent. It must be, that in everything we do we set a high bar. Fragmented, small efforts won't get us far enough.

You see, choosing to prosper means a completely different behaviour from rising. One of the biggest challenges to the euphoria of rising is the distribution of the economic dividend of the rise. Rising improves the fortunes of people who already have the skills and competence to participate in profitable economic activity. The beneficiaries are from all over the world. But to prosper is to see people become economically active to be able to self-actualise and prosper because they met the demand of new economic activity with the skills to fulfil the requirements. To prosper is have the confidence that one has the means to bequeath a better economic outcome to one's child. To rise is to feed today. To prosper is to look beyond current generation!

So, let's not allow our personal success to make us complacent. We have a lot to do. We must create prosperity in each country to build a prosperous continent.

We must continue to work to realise our personal potential and encourage others around us to raise the bar. We have prosperity to create.

I once saw the Heritage Theatre Series production *Wogbejeke*[8]. It is a stage production of the story of the key architects of Ghana. It portrayed two different approaches to the struggle for Ghana's independence. As a business leader, I could see what would drive two different approaches to solving the same challenge. But that was not the message that struck a nerve. I watched the sacrifice of the ordinary Ghanaian. The people for whom this was all too real. The lives lost. And then the victory won for independence.

Then it hit me: perhaps Africa rose a long time ago. Perhaps, just maybe, independence was the real rise. That the domino effect across Africa that followed the momentous change in Ghana was truly the call to a rising continent.

That is when I was saddened. If those adults who patiently and diligently worked for this rise and jubilated at their victory were alive today, what would they say? Is this the Africa of their dreams? Is this the outcome of their rise?

[8] *Wogbejeke* means we have a journey to take, in the Ga language of Southern Ghana

That same day, in the evening, I found myself at Accra Symphony Orchestra's production 'Accra Goes to Opera'. What a magnificent production that was! The talent and the poise that went into such a theatrical production gave me goosebumps. To see all this possible right here in Accra was breathtaking. The production reminded me that there is no talent we cannot find on this continent. The question is whether we will resourcefully nurture talent and allow our people to creatively design a brighter future.

These masterpieces speak of two different worlds in the same place.

One reminds us of where we have come from. The call to rise was acted upon a long time ago.

The other reminds us that, as we look forward to the future, we must build prosperity for our people. Economic prosperity will take our people from surviving life to enjoying the experiences of life. To experience the things that great talent can produce.

So, as we go about our business of leading, let's appreciate the work already done for us and embrace the responsibility to build real prosperity!

For people to thrive, they must move from poverty to prosperity. It is the way it has played out all over the world.

It is also the case that the people in question must be involved in not only the creation of solutions but the delivery of the solutions.

Let us each take the time to really visualise the future continent we want to see and bequeath to future generations. May our visions include the creation of a continent that our future selves will always be proud to belong to.

9

'What we assume is common language sometimes undermines the very speaker.'

INFORMED AND REFORMED LANGUAGE

Our words speak life into our visions. Words are powerful. Really *power-filled.*

Our thoughts make us who we are. Those thoughts are ideas, visions, beliefs and plans that we have. When we speak them, we give life to them. Our words demonstrate our conviction!

But the power of our words is not limited to the direct impact they have on us. Neither are they limited to being positive.

They impact other people. The impact of our words on people depends on the extent to which the person looks up to us; how much weight they place on what we say.

I have had people use their words to tell me I am more than I think I am. People used their words to speak engineering, higher education and leadership into my life. I used my words to speak the same to myself and others.

Words can be negative. I have experienced words that have left me demoralised. The boss who tells you that things simply won't work out for you – even before they have given you a chance! The father who suggests to his child that he lost his job because perhaps he got into a fight which makes it his fault. I have watched a child give up because they were continually reminded that *they can't.*

I wish I could say I always get it right. That I speak only positive hopeful words of myself and others. I don't. Being aware of this means I look out for slip-ups. Whenever possible, I go back to correct things. Because words are powerful!

So, lead with your words!

Our words inform and largely create our mindset: the words we speak ourselves and the words that surround us.

We cannot desire positive outcomes based on our new visions of Africa and constantly focus on discussing negative possibilities. Worse still, possibilities of hopelessness. What we assume is common language sometimes undermines the very speaker!

And, yet, many young Africans continue to feed on negativity. The constant replay of words such as *poor leaders, corrupt, incompetent, not all fingers are made equal* are real examples. Language that creates an excuse for mediocrity by accepting that outcomes for people are set and out of their hands.

Yes, we must have great visions of what we want. More importantly, let those visions influence what we say which will in turn create the right mindset. The right mindset will drive us to action! Action where we collectively create that future we want. We need to reform our language by being informed by our visions!

10

Renewed Mindset

'Choose to be a victor.'

Where are the opportunities in Africa? Well, opportunity finds those who seek it. As my mother always told me, *life is what you make it.*

Someone once asked me how my career had progressed, and the role opportunity has played. I told the person that, at every turn, I have been presented with one or more opportunities.

The real challenge was always with wise discernment.

I remember being in a situation. A professional crossroad. I chose the opportunity that provided less financial benefit but far more learning and growth benefits. Learning and growth mattered more at the time. I knew I needed strength for the leadership journey ahead. I also embraced the fact that my young family needed more of me.

I also recall a time when I completely turned down an opportunity that came with handsome rewards. I had no alternative but knew it was the best choice for my very young family at the time. I had a toddler and another baby on the way.

Purpose, vision, values and priorities help you to wisely discern opportunities. And when we pick which to pursue, we must give it all we have got.

Those choices are sometimes the determinants of whether we are a victim or victor. Why does Africa have so many generational victims? Victimhood passed on from one generation to the next.

The choice typically is a product of socialisation. Socialisation sometimes requires little effort – it is what it is, right? The hard part is changing from victim to victor. The difficulty lies in one word – *mindset.*

Being a *victim* does not necessarily require direct experience. Across the continent, I have met many mental victims – people who live as helpless victims because of what they have been told about themselves and their ancestors. They have allowed words to make them victims without realising it.

Sometimes, it is not ancestors but living relatives who have repeatedly lived as victims and convinced them that there is no hope for their type.

'As for us, we don't like trouble'.
'The masters will come and do it for us'.
'The masters should have stayed and not left, things would be better'.
'My parents are poor. As for us, our portion is poverty'.
'We are helpless, we can't work to fix our situation'.

In one of my talks, I recounted the history of how each of my parents were born into farming families. How they themselves practised farming even as they were being formally educated. I also talked about how much of a dreamer my mother was, growing up. She was victorious in her life situation and decided that there were far greater victories to achieve. I know my victories would not exist without theirs because they gave me permission to think victoriously.

So today, I encourage you to take charge of your mindset. To choose to be a *victor*.

To take charge and create the prosperous Africa you want to see. That prosperity begins with you choosing to live victoriously into your own prosperity. To change your mindset, your language must be reformed to speak positively to your own hearing.

11

'We need systems that create incremental repetitive success.'

BOLD ACTION

We have made it this far. Let's talk about action.

As I think about the willingness to act on change, I reflect on how, each new year, so many people make resolutions. I take my thoughts a step further. People in some parts of Africa acknowledge many changes in time. New week, new month and, of course, new year. This is not dissimilar to the way people on other continents recognise changing seasons of the year.

It is great to celebrate newness. It is tough to act on newness. Change committed to calendar milestones as a way of acknowledging the transition is hard to sustain. The real question is *how do we change these commitments into systemic commitments*?

Every day we read of interventions, donations and support. The story has been the same for decades. So why do outcomes around us seem the same? Why do we still consistently produce need, want and insufficient supply?

It is the system that needs our commitment! Our systems consistently produce the outcomes we see. Don't misunderstand me, there will always be a place for generosity towards each other. But we need systems that give people the highest chance of success. And that starts with each of us.

Charity is not a systemically sustainable solution. It is a tactical fix that relies on emotional conviction of the giver and the robbing of the dignity of the receiver. How can a tactical solution ever deliver development on a large scale?

We need systems that create incremental repetitive success. Repetition creates mastery. We have mastered the systems that create poverty. Let's create and master our own systems for prosperity. As we repeat and master our routines, we are able to positively innovate because a good baseline has been set.

It is time to go back to revisit the notion of pioneering. We need a new generation of pioneers to act. Will we be the pioneers?

When I was a business school student at INSEAD, macroeconomics caught my attention. I was intrigued by the developmental aspects of the course.

It was then that I learnt about Singapore in further detail.

In Ghana, many of us know the story of how at independence Ghana had similar development indices to Singapore. So, what changed?

The people! It was not about natural resources. It was about a generation that decided that the future will be different. Sure, many have argued that the country's strategic position in Asia meant that it had outside support. That is one point of view. But any partnership was predicated on the people's responsibility for change.

They were the pioneer generation of modern Singapore. They are older people now. Pensioners and beyond. I am told when you meet them, you can see the hard work etched on their faces. They gave of themselves to change their country. They ensured that the Singapore we all know and respect today is what it is, through years of hard work of perhaps a whole generation of people.

It is not enough to have great leaders for change. Yes, they are necessary. But work has to be done. The future we want must be created by us. Our visions must be matched by our hard work so that words become action.

Living up to what we believe sometimes means being willing to be set apart. This is particularly true of our values. It is relatively easy to verbalise our values. But they are not true values until they are put to the test.

What do you do, when choosing to stick by your values is the unpopular approach in a situation? What do you do, when choosing your values could cost you in other ways?

Do you let the short-term possible pain get the better of you or do you let the longer-term positive impact of being steadfast sustain you?

Will you be a pioneer ambassador for change? It is time for our visions to influence our language and for our language to change our mindset. A renewed mindset to act on the vision.

12

'Don't confuse humility with mediocrity.'

The Bold New Normal

To be bold we must believe in our greatness!

There is such a wealth of inspiration that has already been created. A great example is the wealth of stories of greatness told in the African Writers' Series.

Those books filled my imagination as a young girl studying literature. The list of great books and authors is endless, and I hope our young people still have the opportunity to study these books. If you have not had the chance to read them, please do.

One of my favourite quotes from Chinua Achebe's *Things Fall Apart* reads: "The lizard that jumped from the high Iroko tree to the ground said he would praise himself if no one else did".

The central character, Okonkwo, said this as he sought to demonstrate his hardworking nature. Confidence and not arrogance.

So, what stops you from expressing your greatness? Do you celebrate your greatness?

You see, the lizard jumping from the high Iroko tree is no mean feat. And this was a source of confidence.

Don't confuse humility with mediocrity.

Right here, on this soil, there is greatness that you should celebrate and use as a foundation to set your sights on higher standards and energise you to achieve greater things.

Indeed, you can; in many ways.

We can in business for a prosperous Africa.

Every business will eventually cease to exist. They either fold or morph into another business. Yet the prosperity of Africa remains tied to business success because the wealth of all nations is tied to business success.

We need leaders and entrepreneurs who see solutions to challenges as business opportunities.

We must create successful businesses that create wealth beyond their founders by providing jobs, innovation and creation opportunities. They cross borders to serve not only their country but other countries too. Most importantly they transcend generations. With each generation their impact becomes greater.

This type of business is a missing ingredient in Africa. It describes what most Africans refer to as *multinationals*. Every multinational has a founder and had a time when it was small.

How many African multinationals do you know of? Are you in business? Do you intend for your company to one day become a multinational? What do you think we need to do to create more of such companies?

We can in technology!

It is time for us to live with bolder drive and be willing to change. Change from economies driven by manual labour to economies driven by technology. Technology is our accelerator!

We must accelerate economic development by using technology to create a multiplier effect.

We are all in. Some of us will create new technologies. Some of us will innovate on existing technologies. Some of us will make better use of technology in our chosen fields of endeavour.

Technology matters to all of us. Let's build our skills in using technology – even the simplest can make a difference.

I try new things a lot. I marvel at the things I discover and learn. All we have to do is try...we must not be afraid to try.

We can in politics!

We must boldly shape our politics away from partisanship to a unifying focus, even in the light of differing ideologies, on bold truly independent outcomes. Which will be the first country to deliver accessibly affordable food for all?

We can for our young leaders!

We need our young people to boldly lead in their spheres of influence.

Ultimately, the Bold New Normal is about creating new visions of Africa, country by country. It is about creating positive mantras to replace diminutive descriptions that undermine positive visions. New mantras that become *langue du jour*! As our daily language builds us up our mindsets will become aligned to our visions. An alignment that will invariably alter our actions.

And when we do this, we will boldly own our own voices and confidently tell our own stories. No longer will discussions be held on Africa with no African present!

It is these *actions* that will ultimately produce **The Bold New Normal** – creating the Africa where everyone prospers!

13

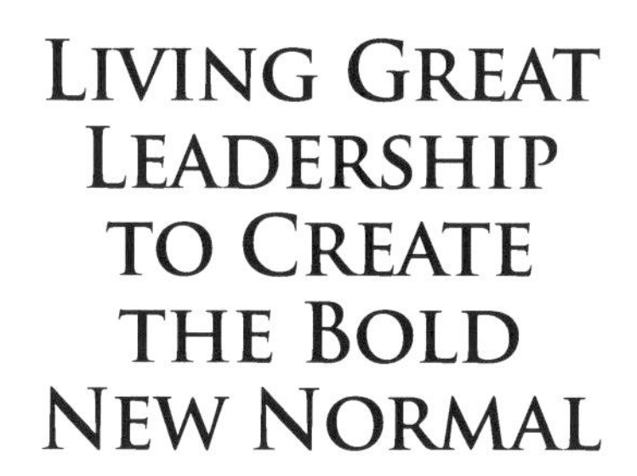

Living Great Leadership to Create the Bold New Normal

'What kind of leader are you and what kind would you like to be?

Leadership from the heart creates greatness. Great leadership happens when other leaders are created because they are inspired by the leader they follow.

But leadership from the heart is probably the toughest way to lead. It demands empathy. It demands walking the talk. It demands knowing when your own concerns do not matter because you have to prioritise the needs and concerns of others.

Leadership from the heart has the potential to create lasting transformational change in the lives of people.

In 2016, the world was challenged to reflect on leadership. The world was watching the USA vote for a new president. When the chips are down, what do people really want in a leader?

Analysing and reflecting on that election refocused my mind on leadership closer to home in to Africa. The greatness of leadership remains one of our biggest debates. We repeatedly hear talk of "if only we had the right leaders, things would be better".

But what this USA election has played out, something I have always known, is that we get the leaders we create. Because the leaders we create are the ones who maybe, just maybe, can present their hearts to us in ways that we believe in. Ways that we can relate to.

So here is the question. *What kind of leadership are we each living? Is it the kind we want reflected back to us?* The way we each live our leadership determines the kind of leadership we find acceptable. It determines the kind of leadership we promote and the kind that ultimately gets to be in front of us.

In the midst of a new type of leadership in the USA, the world is learning new lessons. The USA was playing out one of the greatest dramas of Leadership and Follower-ship of our time. This particular election was not about leadership in the traditional sense. Indeed, while the choice of who to vote for is always somewhat influenced by how much a person is simply liked, this election went all the way to become a popularity contest. A contest of the best showmanship and the ability to pander to insecurities. I doubt the creators of democracy ever thought this was possible.

That ultimately popularity and insecurity could sway an entire election.

Each period has an ability to produce leaders that most closely reflect the period.

African countries have witnessed such leadership at some point in their post-colonial journey. The perils are well known. For me the election demonstrated that electoral choices are not based on a common basis of rationality. In fact, the choice is far less rational and rather emotional. Why? Because we are people. We ultimately choose who we feel the most connection with. And if enough of us feel a connection with the leader on the ballot, we will choose that person.

Over my professional career, I have been led by some great people. I have equally encountered people who are so poor at leading they did not deserve to be called leaders of any form. Poor leaders are noisy, and that noise typically creates chaos.

As I observed the world, here are a few thoughts that came to mind.

Leaders are supposed to amplify the right energy in their followers. When leaders are poor, they focus on amplifying their positional power by driving the most divisive ideas. The ensuing chaos allows them to divide and rule.

Poor leaders distract. Don't allow yourself to be distracted by the noise of poor leadership. Stay focused. Do what is right. Don't spend all your energy arguing for or against. Decide what is right and move on. You have your own future to create. Don't let noise rob you of that.

Watch and learn. People don't become poor leaders because they gained positional power. Power only provides a greater platform for all to see your leadership style.

When leadership is poor, it is an opportunity for followers to demonstrate good leadership.

In some cases in Africa, we have tolerated poor leaders like these for so long. For the first time, at least for some of us, we get to observe from the outside in. Now, perhaps, it is clearer for us to see how some African leadership has been viewed over time from the outside. The image of such leadership in Africa has stuck in global perception despite many countries evolving.

The real challenge is that the rest of the world tends to prefer the sustained narrative of poor leadership in Africa. It creates room for saviours and poor partnership agreements. This is a short-termed historical view of our leaders. What happened to those who led Africans to self-governance? What about the everyday leaders in our society? Discrediting African leadership has become an easy way to discredit all Africans by extension.

We have a unique opportunity to observe and change Africa's narrative by raising the kinds of leaders we want to see. And that starts with us looking in the mirror.

What kind of leader are you and what kind would you like to be?

I am told that intelligence is evenly distributed around the world. However, intelligence and talent need to meet opportunity for us to realise our potential.

Africa, like other parts of the world, has a fair share of great minds. We must create opportunities for them to thrive and prosper. We must also share with them role models and examples they can aspire to become.

We must never forget Wangari Maathai, the environmental political activist who founded the Green Belt movement. We must remind our children of Leymah Gbowee fighting for peace and lifting women up as she rises. Ellen Johnson Sirleaf, not only held her country together through a difficult transition, she continues to be a beacon of light, showing other leaders that it is possible to lead with progressive confidence, no matter what the situation is.

We can and must celebrate people like David Adjaye. He, certainly, is a leading Africa. He is a great architect whose work can be found around the world. We must celebrate Sir Sam Jonah and Shadrack Frimpong. Sir Jonah set a new standard in corporate leadership by leading a home-grown mining company to be listed on the New York Stock Exchange (NYSE). Shadrack, for his part, is our hope! A young man who put the needs of his people above his own. A young man who took his hard-earned prize money as a top graduate and went back to Ghana to establish a school for girls in his home town. All the while putting his own dreams on hold! Their stories inspire us all. We must celebrate leaders like Nelson Mandela in ways that we can actually relate to his sacrifice and achievement. Ways that should inspire us. We must celebrate Denis Mukwege for defying the abusive narrative of his country to lead the healing process for women in his country.

To create new and right leaders, we need representation. Our young people need to see relatable examples of leaders to inspire them into greater action.

What really motivates and drives me is my firm belief that, through business, we *can* transform our continent. Not only do we want to set examples for our people to be entrepreneurial, but we want them to be enterprising on a large scale. We need to mentor our small business owners to grow their enterprises into large businesses – to transform Africa, and, of course, my beloved Ghana, into the amazing place that I believe, and I know, is possible. Let us redefine what is normal in Africa.

Ethical leadership creates prosperity!

Africa's greatest need today is the creation of prosperity. That is the highest priority in the hierarchy of responsibilities. Ethical leadership means a willingness to stand up to responsibility.

Once on a trip to central Accra, I experienced the way I felt when I used to walk those streets as a teenager. I wondered why I would feel that way as I was in a car on the way to a business meeting. And then it struck me – the sights and sounds had not changed so they were tapping into old memories.

How is that possible? How is it possible that, after decades, the place remains the same? How is it that, in real terms, the place has not made tangible progress?

We each have the power to make conscious choices that create prosperity in our sphere of influence. Do you choose to buy a locally-made product over an imported version? The locally produced one sustains jobs locally.

Are you going to be like the science teacher who questioned why children should learn to code or will you be the teacher who encourages discovery?

Do we collectively own the responsibility of making our neighbourhoods progress or should we wait for an official to tell us to do so?

You see, as we lead lives of a high ethical standard, we set the right examples and ensure that leaders of higher standing realise that we will only accept the most ethical behaviour.

The value derived from natural resources must be used judiciously. To do so, we must harness human capital through the right ethical values to create lasting prosperity for all!

Ethical leadership: the confidence to be visible!

To create a generation of great leaders for the future, we need a critical mass of visible ethical leaders today. Leadership visibility can be challenging for some leaders. The ability to reach out to be seen and heard does not come naturally to all. However, as with all skills, this can be taught and learnt.

The real challenge for leadership visibility is ethics. With visibility comes exposure. Exposure not just of what you do professionally as a leader but how you do things. It also shines a light on who you are, your values, choices and consistency.

Future generations need great examples today to tap into and believe in the possibility of their own ability to lead ethically.

I have learnt that, as a leader, all I have done on my life's journey so far is relevant to how I am viewed ethically.

So, today, I encourage you. I encourage you to choose to do what is right even if no one is looking. At the very least, you have an audience of one and what that person thinks of you matters for your future confidence.

Who is a visible and ethical leader you look up to? Why do you look up to them?

Ethical leadership: embrace the right behaviours and develop trust!

As ethical leaders, we must go beyond ourselves to embrace the right behaviours that other people demonstrate around us. We cannot be the only example. By embracing others, we create a critical mass that will influence the wider population.

People doing the right thing need to know that their efforts are noticed and rewarded by leaders. They need to know that they are not alone.

And as we do this, we will create circles of trust. Our development depends on our ability to trust each other to do the right thing.

How do you demonstrate to people that you value the right behaviours they exhibit? Do you trust the people in your circle to be ethical? How can you reinforce that trust?

Ethical leadership: responsibility and accountability!

Ethical leaders take responsibility for the positions they hold. They are willing to be held accountable for their actions.

How do you think these attributes are reflected in leadership today? Is your view a generalised view or is it based on specific examples?

Ethical leaders hold the people they appoint to these standards. They demand that their appointees take responsibility for the positions they hold and are accountable for their actions.

What do responsibility and accountability mean to you? Are you willing to be held to them?

14

When Execution Is Real!

I had the privilege of being part of a team of leaders put together to transform and restore football in Ghana. It was a privilege to work on the restoration of football in Ghana, particularly because it is the national sport. Though the game was not created in Ghana, it has been whole-heartedly adopted by the nation. A nation that has produced many footballing greats who have gone on to create value around the world.

Up until the point of this appointment, my career had

been solely in large multinational organisations. Any public sector engagement I had done as a business leader had been purely at the strategic level. This was my first up close non-private sector operational engagement.

As an association, the Ghana Football Association (GFA) is neither public nor private sector. For the sake of the game, it straddles the two worlds: both private and public sector. Local clubs, on the other hand, should ideally be private entities but still request state support due to local conditions.

It is in this environment that I have had the opportunity to validate many of my ideas on the transformation we need and how this reflects across private and public sector. My experience in football has come to represent a microcosm of how some aspects of our countries work and what we need to make progress.

A number of things have struck me about how we think.

In the first place, we appear to be unwilling to call out bad behaviour of leaders. I am not talking about callouts that are purely emotional rants to occupy airtime. The events that led to the collapse of football were clearly symptomatic of much wider issues within the overall football community. Many of them were issues that people knew about and were willing to call me to explain *what had happened.* These were calls on general malaise; not specific references to the abrupt outcome of mid-2018, but rather what had been happening for years.

I found it surprising that people had deep sequential knowledge of how things were going wrong yet largely remained unwilling to act. We have to learn that we can never hide from our problems. Sticking our head in the sand and hoping that someone else will have the courage to resolve the issues is not the right recipe for our progress.

A few weeks after joining the Normalisation Committee, I was in France at a conference. I got talking to a French lady. As soon as she realised that I was involved with football, she said to me "I knew something was wrong when Ghana did not qualify for the World Cup". In other words, her expectations of Ghana are so high that not making it to the World Cup was counter to her intuition on Ghanaian football.

What I learnt quickly was that, despite the fact that issues are known, we seem to wait for an external, usually non-Ghanaian actor, to take actions that are dramatic. Yes, the GFA belongs to the broader FIFA organisation but did the issues need to get to that point? We failed to take ownership in good enough time. The fact of the matter is that people murmured and muttered but nothing changed.

Secondly, at the inception of the Normalisation Committee, I listened to many public discussions which were about how fit for purpose the Normalisation Team was. I was surprised at how easily we choose to assassinate each other's characters without evidence. In fact, in many cases, the only evidence this character assassination is based on is nationality – the person being *Ghanaian*. Most Africans think of what is local to them as unworthy. The Normalisation Committee could equally have been a team of non-Ghanaians and I suspect that people would have been less emotionally critical.

To my mind, the Normalisation Committee is akin to how in business we engage management consultants to provide a fresh set of eyes to look at our challenges and propose solutions. We don't mind where they are from. Our interest is in how competent they are to deliver on the job. That is what normalisation is about. In many such cases, striking the balance in a diverse team with institutional know-how and independent objective perspectives can create great outcomes.

But our nation hardly focused on this.

There are many other observations on this issue but, perhaps, the strongest indication was the number of bodies within the Ghanaian football community who chose to write to FIFA to share what they thought were valid complaints. This is perhaps the truest indication of a captive mindset. Instead of remaining focused on working with a team of appointed Ghanaians to achieve our collective goals to transform football in Ghana, they focused on reporting externally.

This sort of behaviour continues to demonstrate a lack of maturity in our dealings with each other. What exactly do we expect the others we continue to co-opt to do for us? When will we actively focus on creating our own outcomes? When will we realise that the success of our fellow Ghanaian is our success because individual progress leads to collective progress? When will we truly appreciate that we first need to create and recognise our own local success for the rest of the world to start to see it?

We need to look in the mirror and figure out how we will truly free our minds.

I also observed an orientation away from information, process and order. Looking beyond mindset, I observed a lot about the way we operate.

Operational information seems to be the hardest commodity to gain access to. On the surface, it comes across as a lack of transparency. If it was that simple, we could train people to share. For the most part, however, what is really going on is that we do not place value on information. So, minutes are not systematically filed. People don't keep records, with many taking no notes in meetings they attend. Even when people should have the information, they are quite happy to say they don't know.

The world is in the information age. If we cannot retrieve past information, we must appropriately store current information. We need it for the capacity building I talk about further down.

Then, there comes process. Just simply, *the way things are done.* Too often we assume we should all get lost in routine day to day issues, even when someone is fully employed and is responsible. So, processes break down because they are not consistently followed. You see, in managing the game, our biggest concern should not be about the mundane. Those should happen as a matter of course without senior intervention because the people responsible are honest, transparent and efficient. When they are not honest, transparent and efficient, they cost valuable leadership time spent on minor issue resolution.

Process is the bedrock of consistency. Drawing up plans in advance should become second nature. And when we get the baseline standardised, it creates room for us to think beyond the present. Most importantly, it creates room for leadership to focus on being captains that ethically steer the ship.

Without clear information and process underpinned by timeliness, we struggle to create order. How can we be world-class in any sector without order?

Perhaps most surprising was an inability to engage in constructive debate and teamwork. One of the reasons why companies engage management consultants is that they expect dispassionate objective assessments that lead to new ideas. In order to achieve this, a lot of frank conversations take place where questions are asked and answers are provided. It is about asking honest questions and listening to understand, not to defend a position. This approach is key to innovation and growth in the private sector. It is one of the reasons why companies conduct focus groups or try to understand how other industries work. Most importantly, it is why board membership is diverse and why boardrooms require maturity.

One of my observations was how many times, when people explained a situation or shared their ideas, they seemed to take any follow-on question as a challenge they must defend themselves against. We need to mature beyond the need to permanently defend ourselves. What are we afraid of? No one has a monopoly on knowledge. We need curious and open-minded people who are comfortable with mature debate so the best ideas can bubble to the top of our decision-making tree.

An inability to do this undermines our ability to work as teams. Teams of people focused on common goals and not jostling for personal recognition is what we need across the country. The recognition we need is the collective achievement of our teams. Going with one team member's idea over yours does not make you less smart. In fact, it is a demonstration of smartness if we can recognise ideas that may be better than ours and still have the maturity to pursue the better idea for all.

Questions are not judgements.

We need to develop consistent capacity that creates mastery. The oldest football club in Ghana is over 100 years old. Let that sink in. We have been doing this for over a century. That means our football has seen generations come and go. The question we must ask ourselves is *why have we not mastered something we have done for over a century*? A game that we love and are passionate about.

We need to focus on building our capacity. Capacity built by consistently doing things properly in an orderly manner. We must store and recall information. Information and order will help us to assess what we are doing and identify what we need to improve. Consistency and improvement lead to mastery.

When I posted a graphic of the multi-billion dollar value the English Premier League generates on social media, I thankfully got a good number of responses. But I quickly saw the comments on how this must be created immediately and how such investment must come to our game.

Investment goes to areas where it is most likely to make a good return. Returns don't create themselves. Operating models generate return. So, it does not matter how much we desire to see better economic contributions from any sector – we must put in the hard work consistently to create value.
So, what must we do differently?

Vision
We need to create a clear vision of what football means to us. What is football's role in our progress as a nation? How do we want it to influence what happens domestically? Do we want it to be a permanent positive part of our national brand? These are questions we each must know the answers to in our sectors of operation; and each work hard to realise the visions.

Today the objective of over 90% of our clubs is to sell players. I am not in a hurry to vilify them because they are only doing what almost every sector in Ghana and Africa is doing: largely selling its raw materials, whether human or non-human. Our brightest brains in most fields find no place at home. Our crops find insufficient processing opportunities at home so have to be exported. No sector is exempt.

Our players are the fundamental bearers of the value football can create. Football management must focus on developing and efficiently operating business models that lead to value creation. The value creation cannot just be about discovering the raw material and quickly selling it on for others to add value through great management and extract the most gain. If others have mastered how to manage and create value in football, so can we – regardless of the gap that may exist today. We must have the confidence to self-actualise like any other human being.

Mindset

Our mindset remains our biggest collective challenge. We must liberate our minds enough to believe in greater visions of our future. A future that looks nothing like our today. A future that we should be able to create. Imagine a world where every household in the world that loves football is willing to tune into the Ghanaian local game for the most captivating experience? Imagine a world where people say, "Ghanaians learn to play football before they learn to walk", as someone once told me mythically about Brazilians? We must bring our minds to believe in such a world.

Behaviour

Our behaviour must start to reflect a focus on the vision. Our discussions in the media have to rise above pettiness to taking a critical look at issues, maturely debating pros and cons with a view to contribute positively. We need behaviours that encourage people who participate in realising the vision. Our general discourse and behaviours must reflect our positive belief in the visions we are creating.

Action

Our behaviour should ultimately lead us to tirelessly take action – consistently. The transformation we need is not a onetime event. Nor is it a destination. It is a change we make to be different and always strive to excel through our actions.

I hope this chapter brings my thoughts on **The Bold New Normal** to life for you. As we have these conversations we must also plan to act. To do the work that may take an entire generation to create a country our future Ghanaians deserve.

And maybe, just maybe, our nations can become the beacons that they rightly should be.

15

CONCLUSION

I was once in a business meeting when a leader was asked by a colleague what his proudest business achievement was in recent times. He thought for a moment and said *nothing!*

I was astounded. Here I was in a powerful meeting and because this powerful man could not articulate achievements in financial terms, he said he was proud of nothing. Yet I knew for a fact that his business had positively touched many lives.

That, if he was proud of nothing else, he could be proud of that.

That really sums up how we have allowed business to evolve in our world. Business has come to mean a set of quantitative metrics that determine our performance. Anything less is not worthwhile.

My interest in taking a bold new approach to creating prosperity was born out of my personal experiences. As described, the stark contrast of living a middle-class life in the UK to arriving in Ghana at one of the country's lowest economic points left an indelible mark on me. Life experiences have ways of doing that to a person.

It was an emotional experience. On the one hand were positive emotions of engaging with children who looked like me. They may not have sounded like me, but they certainly were open to all that is me. On the other hand, hardship. Why should food be a challenge? Why should my parents have such a hard time providing for us? Granted, it was a national issue, but our experiences are always personal, especially being too young to process anything that occurred on a national scale. It was an age when news was still a programme that was out of my consideration set!

Those emotions undoubtedly created enduring memories – etched in my conscience forever.

Slowly, but surely, those memories started to inform my perception of the world. Still the world that was within my reach, my local world, but the change was happening around me.

Given the context, I deeply cared about the suffering others were experiencing. Suffering that was far worse than what I might have complained about. I heard of deaths from eating poisonous food like inedible cassava substitutes. I wonder whether anyone had ever measured the developmental delay babies and toddlers of the time must have suffered. Reflecting on this as I type breaks my heart.

And, so, my heart has been conditioned to care about disadvantage. A lot of disadvantage around the world is structural. We have created a world where some people are structurally disadvantaged.

My conviction is that leaders, particularly in business, have a role to play in changing those structures. Yes, we can make better decisions for our businesses to impact society for good. But there is more. As a business leader, I realise that it is beyond decision; it is rather a choice. A choice to serve the communities we work in. Service to people is service we will still make sustainable profits from. Profits that sustain not only the cash investor but society at large which is equally an investor.

Business leaders need to be bold. Business leadership has to go beyond direct and immediate performance to focus more on progress. How much has this business contributed to moving society forward?

What I speak of is transformative change and not just incremental change. Transformation requires courage. Courage that says I am willing to create a different future because I see it in my mind's eye, and I am sure it is a better future.

We must retrain leaders in this imperative. An imperative that places their responsibility, by virtue of the positions they hold, on a much higher moral level than has previously been assumed. We have to re-orient them to the realisation that their positions are not just for their immediate direct shareholders who own the business but for stakeholders whose existence are impacted by their business.

Today, technology affords us a level of transparency in information sharing that has never been seen before. Awareness of impact is prescient in the mind. But what purpose is the business and its leadership serving?

We can't wait for government because government alone no longer has power in that way. Yet, good governance remains a necessary foundation. Today many governments find themselves beholden to populations influenced by technology companies.

Business is now the biggest platform in the world and leaders wield the leverage.

Business was created for prosperity. Business knows the model of how to create prosperity. So how will business now integrate humanity, nature, technology and known business principles to chart a new purposeful role that makes businesses better stewards of our world? Our quest to create the bold new normal must be executed in the context of a new world business is leading us to. In riding the business wave to make our visions relevant, we will create the true prosperity of our continent.

Printed in Great Britain
by Amazon